SpringerBriefs in Law

SpringerBriefs present concise summaries of cutting-edge research and practical applications across a wide spectrum of fields. Featuring compact volumes of 50 to 125 pages, the series covers a range of content from professional to academic. Typical topics might include:

- A timely report of state-of-the art analytical techniques
- A bridge between new research results, as published in journal articles, and a contextual literature review
- A snapshot of a hot or emerging topic
- A presentation of core concepts that students must understand in order to make independent contributions

SpringerBriefs in Law showcase emerging theory, empirical research, and practical application in Law from a global author community. SpringerBriefs are characterized by fast, global electronic dissemination, standard publishing contracts, standardized manuscript preparation and formatting guidelines, and expedited production schedules.

Simona Strungaru

The Hidden Child Brides of the Syrian Civil War

Vulnerable and Voiceless in Human Rights Law and Practice

Springer

Simona Strungaru
School of Humanities, Arts and Social Sciences
University of New England
Armidale, NSW, Australia

ISSN 2192-855X ISSN 2192-8568 (electronic)
SpringerBriefs in Law
ISBN 978-981-97-2158-0 ISBN 978-981-97-2159-7 (eBook)
https://doi.org/10.1007/978-981-97-2159-7

This Springer imprint is published by the registered company Springer Nature Singapore Pte Ltd.
The registered company address is: 152 Beach Road, #21-01/04 Gateway East, Singapore 189721, Singapore

Foreword

What happens to a young girl's life when she is left homeless, stateless, and married? Almost all the world considers child marriage an insidious practice—but why does it still occur, and is it possible the practice is increasing? This book, *The Hidden Child Brides of the Syrian Civil War: Vulnerable and Voiceless in Human Rights Law and Practice* by Simona Strungaru, who has spent half her life living in the Middle East, seeks to explain how international law and the international community have failed to protect vulnerable girls and end the practice of child marriage. It does so via the lens of Syrian refugee child brides living in Jordan. This lens allows the spotlight to be shone on the historical, cultural, social, economic, political, and religious reasons that contribute to the perpetuation of child marriage practices. While the practice is applicable to both boys and girls, it is girls who are most affected and impacted. This book seeks to understand not only why child marriage continues, but what are the effects and impacts of child marriage on young girls. This book offers an important discussion of child marriage within the context of refugee studies and refugee law, and more broadly, the intersections between Western and Arab law, within which gaps are allowing child marriages to continue.

Sadly, the COVID-19 pandemic has produced more victims. In recent years, the COVID-19 pandemic has brought about economic downturns and interruptions to social services, including education, impacting the lives of vulnerable children, and their health and socio-economic status. Education is a key factor when it comes to preventing child marriages. Families make decisions about a girl's education and marriage in *parallel*. When schooling is no longer considered viable, child marriage increasingly becomes an option to decrease a family's burden.

In writing this foreword, I do so as a researcher of refugee rights and policy over some 20 years. In 2005, I co-edited a book with Prof. John Minns and Prof. Andrew Wells, titled, *Seeking Refuge: Asylum Seekers and Politics in a Globalising World*. The aim of this edited collection was to demonstrate that the tragedy facing refugees in recent decades was because of government policy and ineffective international laws. We argued that people do not flee their homes, jobs, schools, universities, communities, and places of worship and comfort easily. To leave behind that which is familiar—language and culture—is a step many in the West can't imagine having to contemplate. In the case of child brides, it is their sense of 'not-belonging' in law and being invisible to the public eye, that their vulnerability is even further compounded.

In the 2005 book, we blamed local elites, dictators, and ethnic haters for the millions of personal tragedies which made up the refugee 'crisis'. We also recognised the contributions of insensitive governments, willing to ignore international law and allow refugees to drown at sea, be detained in detention camps on Australian soil, and be returned home to likely face death—those we determined by very arbitrary means to be not entitled to our protection as refugees. They did this to win elections on the back of fear and loathing. The book was largely inspired by the events of August 2001, when the Liberal-National Government led by John Howard refused entry into Australian waters of the Norwegian freighter the MV *Tampa.* The *Tampa* has rescued 433 asylum seekers from a sinking fishing boat in international waters. The asylum seekers were mostly Hazaras, an ethnic minority from Afghanistan. The decision occurred two months before the general election at which the Howard government was seeking re-election. The *Tampa* Captain, Arne Rinnan, ignored the Howard Government's command to not enter Australian waters and, as a result, the freighter was boarded by the Australian military special forces. Within days the Howard Government introduced the Border Protection Bill into the Australian parliament citing Australian sovereignty as a means of determining who could enter Australia. This was echoed at the subsequent federal election in which the Howard Government declared, 'we decide who comes into this country and the circumstances in which they come'.

The Howard government was returned to power. But not before they accused asylum seekers en route to Australia on 7 October 2001 of throwing their children overboard in order to receive and implement favourable refugee decisions. This followed the SIEV-X event. The impersonal SIEV-X acronym stands for 'suspected illegal entry vessel'. The vessel was a fishing boat en route from Indonesia to Australia carrying some 400 asylum seekers. On 19 October 2001, it sank south of Java killing 353 people, mostly women and children. On the back of the events, motivated by political ends, asylum seekers continue to be vulnerable and voiceless. This is more so when it comes to children, who are transited to other countries by their parents yet are subject to the consequences of that transition, as in the case of child refugee brides.

My own experiences of the refugee 'crisis' occurring in Australia in 2001 were vastly different from those of many others. I spent that summer at Villawood Immigration Detention Centre in New South Wales, Australia, with my son visiting asylum seekers who were held in mandatory detention while their asylum seeker status was determined. Many languished there for years, waiting for decisions that in some cases never came, returned to their homelands, facing unknown horrors and fear—many were never heard of again. One was a young Iranian girl called Mena. I spent a few afternoons with her—she was smart, inquisitive, open, and trusting. When her family returned to Iran, I lost contact with them. It is in my worst nightmares that I wonder what happened to her. It is based on these experiences that Simona Strungaru's book reminds us that voiceless girl brides do not have to be hidden and silent.

I am also reminded of my own privileged position as a young, white woman growing up in Australia in the 1970s. As with many others of a generation, we were warned of 'stranger danger'. We soon realised, though, that the threat of harm and violence came from those closest to us—fathers, stepfathers, uncles, grandparents, and our teachers. We, however, could speak out against the violence, though we may not have always done so then. We also were not forced to marry those who raped us, though some may have been. We also understood, if not then, but now, that we have human rights and a voice that demands those rights be recognised, if only too late. We also learnt that the scars of childhood violence did not have to destroy us, rather it could make us stronger and fiercer. I wish this strength for my sisters in the world, however, I fear for them, while governments, the world, and the media, ignore their plights and the tragedy of being a child bride.

Armidale, Australia

Associate Professor Jo Coghlan

Preface

I was living in Saudi Arabia when the Syrian Civil War erupted in 2011. Although Saudi Arabia was one of the very few states in the region that was relatively unaffected by the political upheavals of the Arab Spring that were occurring in the neighbouring states, tensions, fears, and anxieties were nonetheless felt by all. This was especially true for my Syrian friends, neighbours, and colleagues in Saudi Arabia, who watched from afar as their homeland descended further into chaos with each passing day. Every day we watched in horror news of the atrocities being inflicted on innocent civilians, including children, particularly by insurgent militant Islamic terrorist groups. I did not have one Syrian friend who was not personally affected by the civil war—their families were killed, and their hometowns were destroyed. Those living abroad had no home to return to, many of them becoming essentially stateless. To this day, my Syrian friends have been uprooted, struggling to find a new home to 'belong' to and provide a safe environment to raise their children. No-one in the world deserves to endure the pain of having everything they loved and cherished be *forcibly* taken away from them.

The Syrian Civil War has since been deemed one of the worst humanitarian crises of the twenty-first century. Unprecedented political, social, and economic instability in Syria continues to undermine all aspects of human security for the Syrian population. Caught in the literal crossfire of a multifaceted and multi-sided political war, Syrian children, in particular, have been adversely affected on an unprecedented scale as a result of this conflict. As Syrian refugee and education activist, Muzoon Almellehan (2023, p. 1)[1] describes, 'one day you're a kid playing sports and watching cartoons. The next day there is war, and you have to leave for a refugee camp'. For many Syrian children, conflict, displacement, fear, and uncertainty is all they have ever known. Since 2011, more than half a million Syrians are estimated to have been killed, and over 12 million displaced since the start of the war.

Forced to leave their homes, and seek protection and humanitarian assistance in neighbouring countries, the refugee's journey to safety and security is perilous and often unreachable. This is especially true for refugee children. Often separated

[1] Almellehan, M. (2023). *Muzoon: A Syrian Refugee Speaks Out.* USA: Alfred A. Knopf.

from their families, with little or no documentation, refugee children all too often become victims to violence, abuse, and exploitation, particularly within precarious liminal environments like refugee camps. It was in 2014, however, that I realised how truly dire the situation for refugee Syrian children, particularly girls, really was, and continues to be. In a report by the BBC titled the *Untold misery of child brides*,[2] I read of Syrian refugee girls forced into marriages in Jordan as a copying mechanism for the girl's families. These girls are sold like a product at the mall to wealthy buyers 'shopping' around and preying on desperate Syrian refugee families.

I was shocked and curious to get to the bottom of why this was happening, and what is being done to protect refugee children from exposure to this nefarious practice. This book is the result of that research. What I found was that this harmful practice was not unique to Syrian refugees in Jordan. Rather, the practice of child marriage occurs worldwide, threatening the lives and futures of millions of children.

Using a sociolegal approach, the aim of this book is to provide a human-centred interrogation of contemporary international and regional human rights protections (or lack thereof) in place for those most vulnerable and voiceless against the practice of forced child marriage. With a specific focus on Syrian refugee children this book sets out to, firstly, conceptualise the practice—its reasons and its impacts on children. Secondly, the book aims to contextualise the practice within Syria's host neighbouring state, Jordan. Thirdly, the book aims to interrogate the effectiveness of international human rights laws in protecting refugee children from child marriage, and its application within the Middle Eastern region, generally, and within Jordan, specifically.

The term 'refugee' has become a powerful label of the modern era that both 'stereotypes and institutionalises a status' (Zetter, 1988, p. 1).[3] While international human rights law and refugee studies alike contribute to understanding the impacts and significance of conflicts and disasters on the lives of individuals and communities, these interpretations are often highly politicised, with individual-states often dependent on their own restrictive criteria in identifying those in most need of protection. As a result, those most vulnerable may often consequently become overlooked within laws and public policy, thereby exacerbating their state of vulnerability. This continues to be the case for Syrian refugee children.

Despite being internationally recognised as a human rights violation, refugee girls continue to be let down by gendered international and national laws that deny them protection, largely because of social and cultural norms, and customary traditions.

[2] BBC News. (2014, Aug 20). *Syrian conflict: Untold misery of child brides*. Retrieved from: https://www.bbc.com/news/world-middle-east-28250471.

[3] Zetter, R. (1988). Refugees and refugee studies a label and an agenda. *Journal of Refugee Studies, 1*(1), 1–6.

I hope this book further highlights the need for urgent and effective national and international responses. Because every child deserves to be happy. Because every child deserves the right to be heard and be protected. Because one case of sexual violence against a child is one too many.

Armidale, Australia Simona Strungaru

Praise for *The Hidden Child Brides of the Syrian Civil War*

"This insightful and empathetic study into the nefarious global practice of child marriages is important reading for those seeking to understand this contemporary issue. The case study of child marriage in Syrian refugee populations languishing in refugee camps in Jordan highlights the impacts of this pernicious activity, as well as the need for urgent national and international response. The book is especially timely for those working in the field seeking to identify possible mechanisms for leverage in order to stop this abusive practice, and for this, the author is to be congratulated".

—Dr. Johanna Garnett, *Senior Lecturer in Sociology and Peace Studies, University of New England, Armidale*

Contents

Chapter 1
Introduction: The Middle East Refugee Diaspora and Its Liminality

Abstract Human history is deeply rooted in diaspora (Bae et al. in Science 358(6368), 2017 [5]). Although history has often represented change and migration as inevitable cultural phenomena, particularly with the advent of large-scale globalisation, the physical uprooting and exodus of populations is perhaps occurring now in the twenty-first century more than ever before.

Human history is deeply rooted in diaspora [5]. Although history has often represented change and migration as inevitable cultural phenomena, particularly with the advent of large-scale globalisation, the physical uprooting and exodus of populations is perhaps occurring now in the twenty-first century more than ever before. According to Bakewell [6] and Zetter [43], however, it is important to clearly distinguish between patterns and events of 'forced' versus 'voluntary' migration. The subsequent establishment of 'refugee studies' as a formal field of scholarship in the 1980s sought to distinguish between these concepts and map some of its boundaries, by excluding patterns of migrations largely caused by "self-determined decisions" (Zetter [43], p. 5, see also Bloch [7]; [6]). In 2005, Director of the Department of International Protection from the UN High Commissioner for Refugees, Erika Feller, emphasised the importance of this distinction, stating "refugees are not migrants" ([12], p. 27).

The nature of the mass exodus of populations witnessed in the present day significantly relates to the forced removal or evacuation of individuals from their home or country of origin, commonly due to armed conflicts or natural disasters. According to data provided by the United Nations High Commissioner for Refugees (UNHCR) [37], at the end of 2022, for the first time on record, a staggering figure of more than 108 million people forcibly displaced due to conflict and violence, persecution, and human rights violations was documented. This figure was largely propelled by the ongoing war in Ukraine, as well as re-emerging or protracted conflicts in Myanmar, Afghanistan, and numerous African states, such as Ethiopia, Burkina Faso, Nigeria, and the Democratic Republic of Congo [37]. As United Nations' High Commissioner for Refugees, Filippo Grandi, asserted, this stark figure is "sobering and alarming in equal measure" and "a record that should never have been set"

S. Strungaru, *The Hidden Child Brides of the Syrian Civil War*,
SpringerBriefs in Law, https://doi.org/10.1007/978-981-97-2159-7_1

[35]. This data is certainly reflective of Palestinian-American scholar, Edward ([25], p. 173), introduction to the concept 'exile' within his essay, *Reflections on Exile*, as both "strangely compelling to think about but terrible to experience". It is the 'universality', rather than the "'uniqueness' of the refugee phenomena" that seemingly characterises modern-day displacement ([43], p. 4). Although Zetter [43] presented his discussion on the refugee phenomena 35 years ago, his remarks nonetheless remain pertinent in the present day as the global community continues to deal with "general issues not just unique and particular instances" (p. 4),these issues "encompass longer term issues of resettlement and assimilation" (p. 1). Similarly, Said ([25], p. 174) relevantly postulated at the turn of the century that the current age—"with its modern warfare, imperialism, and the quasi-theological ambitions of totalitarian rulers—is indeed the age of the refugee, the displaced person, mass immigration".

Characteristically, what Said [25] refers to as the 'age of the refugee' represents more than just the literal journey of geographical relocation. It represents the severing of peoples from "their roots, their land, their past" ([25], p. 177). Within his essay, Said ([25], p. 173) intensely evokes imagery of 'exile' as "the unhealable rift forced between a human being and a native place, between the self and its true home". Here, Said beckons his readers to empathise with "its essential sadness" that "can never be surmounted" ([25], p. 173). In the same vein, French philosopher Weil ([41], p. 40) in her book *The Need for Roots*, explores the complexities of 'rootedness', suggesting that one's need to be rooted to a place is perhaps, above all, "the most important and least recognised need of the human soul". Weil ([41], p. 40) broadly defines 'roots' as being inextricably linked to a human being's

> … active and natural participation in the life of a community which preserves in living shape certain particular treasures of the past and certain particular expectations for the future. This participation is a natural one, in the sense that it is automatically brought about by place, conditions of birth, profession and social surroundings. Every human being needs to have multiple roots. It is necessary for him to draw wellnigh the whole of his moral, intellectual and spiritual life by way of the environment of which he forms a natural part.

In this way, the refugee is, thus, more than a literal figure of displacement. Rather, the body of the refugee represents the "perilous territory" of liminality and not-belonging to neither place nor people ([25], p. 140).

The peril realities of displacement are, perhaps, none more pertinent and familiar to the ethnic Arab majority refugees of the Middle East and North Africa. The Middle East has been the "scene of continuous forced migration over the past 150 years" ([10], p. 1). The diasporic flow of civilians has been for some time a defining feature of life in the Middle East that "indelibly mark the landscape" ([10], p. 24). In 2022, the UNHCR recorded 16 million forcibly displaced individuals in the Middle East and North Africa, including refugees, internally displaced persons (IDPs), asylum seekers, and stateless persons [34]. Of this number, around 2.2 million displaced persons were school-aged [34]. The interconnectedness of the Middle Eastern states with its shared borders, as well as, a shared sense of identity and culture amongst the Arab peoples, marks the Middle East a significant region as both a source and host of displacement. With regard to the latter, data provided by the UNHCR ([37], p. 2) revealed that, globally, 70% of refugees and other people in need of international protection in 2022 were hosted in neighbouring countries. According to the UNHCR ([37], p. 2), Lebanon and Jordan hosted the largest number of displaced persons in the Middle East, relative to their national populations, with Lebanon hosting 1 in 7, and Jordan hosting 1 in 16, displaced persons (UNHCR [37], p. 2).[1]

While 'war' and 'poverty' are frequently cited causes for human displacement and mobility, the large-scale displacement continuing to occur in the Middle East raises fundamental questions concerning political systems of power and authority in the region [4]. Two significant events that have led to the mass exodus of populations in the twentieth century largely centre on state formation and/or the external intervention by foreign powers in regional affairs. The first event was the post-World War I de facto division of the Kurdistan territory into the modern states of Türkiye, Iraq, Iran, and Syria, which was formalised by the 1923 Lausanne Peace Treaty [3]. The division of Kurdistan occurred following the collapse of the Ottoman Empire when efforts by Kurdish nationalists to establish an autonomous state were rebutted by the United Kingdom in an attempt to 'appease' the newly formed post-war Kemalist government of the Republic of Türkiye [3]. As a result, Kurds have faced persecution and marginalisation within these four states, and are, presently, one of the world's largest stateless ethnic groups [11]. The second prominent event of displacement that occurred in the mid-twentieth century in the Middle East was the 1948 Palestinian exodus during the Arab–Israeli war. The expulsion of more than 700,000 Arab Palestinians occurred after the United Nations adopted the 'Partition Resolution' in 1947 which set out to demarcate and establish two separate states—Jewish and Arab—on the one land in response to the WWII Holocaust [13]. Hostilities between the Jews and Arabs, however, subsequently culminated after Israel declared independence in 1948, causing two-thirds of the Palestinian people to become refugees [26]. According to the organisation 'Human Rights Watch', "there are more than 5.9 million Palestinian refugees, including the descendants of those who fled or were expelled" in the world today ([26], online). Furthermore, subsequent conflicts since the late twentieth-century such as the invasions of Afghanistan (1999–2021) and Iraq (2003–2011) by United States of America-led coalition, and most recently, the Arab Spring and 2011 Syrian revolution, continue to markedly influence regional dynamics within the Middle East, and present significant challenges to addressing human rights and humanitarian responses. In the words of Said ([25], p. 174), these events illustrate that 'exile' is, for the most part, "produced by human beings for other human beings".

The effects of forced displacement and refugee resettlement for both displaced nations and individuals, as well as, for host nations is exhaustive and devasting. The impacts of forced displacement on individuals are multidimensional and may have significant long-term effects on socioeconomic development ([8], p. 6). Broadly, forced displacement contributes to adverse effects on physical and mental health, due

---

[1] This statistic does not include the presence of Palestinian refugees in Lebanon and Jordan. "When 487,300 Palestine refugees in Lebanon and 2.4 million Palestine refugees in Jordan registered with UNRWA are included, the proportions in Lebanon and Jordan increase to 1 in 4" (UNHCR 2022, p. 3).

to lack of access to health services, and unsanitary housing and encampment conditions, mal- or under-nutrition, as well as, increased risk of communicable diseases, including increased risk of sexually transmitted infections (STIs) [8]. The stress and trauma of forced displacement, and associated disruption of the social environment and separation from home and family, may also cause mental health illnesses, such as, anxiety, depression, and trauma [8]. As well, forced displacement significantly impacts an individual's access to basic infrastructure and services, housing, security, employment opportunities and income, and education [8]. For children especially, displacement contributes to an increased risk of vulnerability to exploitation and abuse, particularly due to the fact that children often become separated from their families whilst fleeing their homes [8]. As will be comprehensively presented throughout this book, children's separation from their families, lack of identity documentation, and exposure to increased stress and financial strain on displaced children's families that often result in extreme poverty, are significant risk factors for child marriage.

As noted nearly 30 years ago, the Arab identity or 'Arabness' continues to be "constantly reinvented and…threatened" ([27], 11). For the Middle Eastern refugee, culture has remained one of the few tangible links between them and 'soil', in place of the "ordinary loyalties of citizenship" from their homeland ([21], p. 32). Consequently, displacement events often result in what Said [25] and Malkki [21] infer as a 'pathologisation' of homelessness—that is, a condition in which "the orderliness of the transplantation disappears" ([21], p. 34). What this suggests is that the refugee, as a liminal "naked unaccommodated" personae, may no longer feel themselves bound by ethical and moral precepts in situations of crisis and displacement (Turner [31], cited in Malkki [21], p. 34). The issue of child marriage among Syrian refugee populations in Jordan may be seen to arguably reflect such a condition occurring within the crevasses of transnational jurisdictions. As will be discussed, the intersectionality of child marriage within these vulnerable environments consequently affects a child's access to fundamental human rights and their ability to secure a livelihood.

1.1 The Syrian Civil War: Causes and Consequences

In his text, *Syria in Ruins*, Sorenson ([28], p. 1) takes his readers on an imaginative journey to Damascus—"one of the oldest continuously inhabited cities in the world" located in the "heart of a rich and complex civilization called Syria". Sorenson describes Syria's "deep roots in antiquity" whose "neighbourhoods seem unchanged since the seventh century", with its gothic walls, stone streets, ancient architecture, and souqs brimming with the aromas and flavours of spices and produce ([28], p. 1). Since 2011, however, a land that once evoked ancient civilizations, culture, and language, has come to be associated with images of 'civil war', 'devastation', and 'the Islamic State' [28]. The year 2011 significantly marks the moment in history in which Syria was plunged into a civil war that "has created the largest refugee and displacement crisis of our time, affecting millions of people and spilling into surrounding countries" ([42], online). In a statement released in 2023, UN Special Envoy to Syria, Geir Pedersen, declared that the current scale of humanitarian assistance needed in Syria is at its highest point since the start of the conflict, with record levels of poverty, food insecurity, and breakdown of basic services due to a "burgeoning economic crisis" noted ([40], online).

The Syrian civil war markedly occurred after a revolutionary wave of protests swept through numerous countries in the Middle East, now referred to as the 'Arab Spring'. The Arab Spring began in December 2010 with the self-immolation of a 26-year-old Tunisian fruit merchant in condemnation to national corruption [18]. His act consequently spurred an unprecedent uprising by the people in Tunisia demonstrating against the oppressive government and poor national living standards within Tunisia [18, 19]. What began as a local demonstration in Tunisia, however, quickly echoed into a causal sequence of mass social protests for democratisation and justice throughout the repressed Middle East and North Africa region [20, 22]. These protests were the accumulation of antagonism and frustration against authoritarian and corrupt rulers and regimes whereby freedom for rights and economic opportunities, and importantly, democracy, was demanded [20]. While these protests led to the collapse of longstanding authoritarian governments in some states within the region, including Tunisia, Libya, Egypt, and Yemen, other neighbouring states like Syria fought for the survival of authoritarianism [4].

Inspired by news of the region's revolutions previously thought to be 'unthinkable', 15 teenage boys spray-painted anti-regime graffiti on a school wall in the city of Dara'a, Syria, that read, "It's your turn, doctor!"—a reference to Syrian President Bashar al-Assad's previous career [19, 30]. These actions led to the boys' arrest and torture. Syrian civilians rallying behind the boys began protesting more 'modest' actions by the government that called for greater freedoms, an end to corruption, and the release of political prisoners [19]. Violence, however, rapidly escalated when security services were directed by President Assad to "put down the protests with force", resulting in the deaths of dozens of protestors in an open fire in Dara'a ([19], online). Hereafter, protests "quickly took on a revolutionary nature" across Syria with citizens calling for the removal of the Assad Government ([2], online). By the summer of 2011, Syria had descended into a civil war involving several armed factions. The civil war was fought primarily between the forces of the Ba'athist Syrian Arab Republic led by President Bashar al-Assad and its allies, and splintered opposition and rebel groups, including the Free Syrian Army (primarily defectors from Assad's army), and the majority-Kurdish Syrian Democratic Forces (SDF) [19, 20]. Concerningly, Salafi (Sunni Muslim) Jihadist Groups, such as, Jabhat al-Nusra Front, and designated terrorist extremist organisations,[2] such as, the Islamic State (also known as the 'Islamic State of Iraq and the Syria' (ISIS)) emerged, whose members consisted largely of remnant al-Qaeda militants "eager to capitalise on Syria's chaos" ([19], online). Taking advantage of the conflict, and exploiting destabilised localities within Syria, the Islamic State inflicted brutality and destruction on

[2] Listed according to Bureau of Counterterrorism of the U.S. Department of State. Retrieved 15 July 2023, from: https://www.state.gov/foreign-terrorist-organizations/.

majority civil targets in order to gain power and control and establish themselves as a caliphate in the Levant [28]. As time progressed, the Syrian war became more than just an internal conflict between the Assad regime and anti-government opposition groups. Rather, the Syrian war became a strategic site of prolonged political and military dispute involving multiple key technologically advanced regional and international powers, including Russia and Iran, on one side (backing the Assad Government), and the USA, United Kingdom, France, Saudi Arabia, and Türkiye, on the other side (backing anti-government groups) [9, 28]. As a result, the situation became irrefutably complex—politically, socially, and geographically.

Much like the season of spring which is typically associated with 'joy' and 'renewal', so too, the Arab Spring emerged out of the need to institute a regional counter-authoritarian political and social 'renewal' [14]. There have been few countries that have undergone so much wide scale destruction from the Arab Spring, however, like Syria [28]. As of 2023, the conflict in Syria is now in its twelfth year. While the war has, overall, settled into a stalemate with the Assad Government securing power and regaining control of most of the country, intermittent fighting continues to occur, particularly in northwest Syria (Al [2]). As the longest and most devastating crisis of the Arab Spring [1], Syria presently faces profound economic hardships, limited political progress, security uncertainty, and the largest displacement crisis in the world [38]. In March 2023, the Syrian Observatory for Human Rights [29] estimated that more than 600,000 people have been killed since the start of the war. Additionally, a total of nearly 13 million people—more than half of Syria's pre-war population—are currently displaced, with 6.9 million internally displaced persons, and 5.4 million refugees [38]. Of the number of Syrian refugees, more than 2.6 million are children [33]. In 2022, Syrian refugees accounted for almost 1 in 5 of the total number of refugees globally, with many living in refugee camps and informal settlements, and more than 77% residing in host neighbouring communities, including Türkiye, Lebanon, Jordan, and Iraq [37]. Meanwhile, at the start of 2023, a 7.8 magnitude earthquake struck northwest Syria and southeast Türkiye which further exacerbated the economic and humanitarian crisis in the region, impacting close to 18 million people [24]. According to the UN Under-Secretary-General for Humanitarian Affairs and Emergency Relief, Griffiths [15], 90% of the Syrian population has been pushed below the poverty line since the start of the civil war, and 70% are in dire need of humanitarian assistance, unable to meet their basic needs [40].

The crisis continues to have significant political, social, economic, and security implications, both nationally and regionally. UNICEF [33] also emphasised that "the economic crisis is worsening negative coping mechanisms and particularly affecting female-headed households"; this is particularly contributing "to the normalization of gender-based violence and child exploitation". As such, children are at particular risk of violence, exploitation, and abuse, and are more frequently being forcibly recruited into armed groups, and forced into labour and early marriage [33]. It is for this reason that this book specifically undertakes a sociolegal exploration of child marriage amongst the Syrian refugee cohort, seeking to contribute to addressing this grave human rights issue.

1.1.1 Jordan's Humanitarian Response

The present-day Syrian humanitarian crisis caused by the prolonged civil war, as well as, ongoing fighting and the recent natural disaster, has caused a large number of Syrian civilians to seek protection, and humanitarian assistance and asylum, in neighbouring countries such as Türkiye, Lebanon, Iraq, and Jordan. Unlike countries such as Lebanon and Iraq where their own political and socio-economic strains have been exacerbated as a result of the Syrian Civil War, particularly in relation to existing sectarian fissures that have overlapped with the "increasingly sectarian alignment of different groups in Syria", Jordan has sought, for the most part, to avoid such divisions and "take a more neutral public stance on Syria" ([17], p. 6).

Jordan is a small semi-arid Arab state bordering the Dead Sea and the Jordan River that separates it from the Palestinian (West Bank) territories and Israel. Its neighbours also include Syria in the north, Iraq in the northeast, and Saudi Arabia in the east and south of the country. For those Syrians seeking a secure life, the political stability of Jordan as well as the close historical, cultural, and geographical relationship shared between both nations are factors that have facilitated a large number of Syrian asylum seekers into Jordan [23]. In addition to its close proximity, Jordan has also been reputed as "the country closest to Syria in social, religious and economic terms" offering refugees the prospect of some of the freedoms that they may have enjoyed in their home country, as well as the "presence of relatives and friends" ([23], p. 1).

Although the total population in Jordan is only around 10 million, Jordan is renowned for its "long-standing hospitality" towards those seeking refuge ([36], p. 4); it is the second largest refugee-hosting nation in the world on a per capita basis [36]. Since the outbreak of the Syrian war, however, more than 1.3 million Syrians have sought refuge in Jordan [16]. As of 2022, there are over 760,000 registered refugees in Jordan, 85.5% of whom are Syrian nationals [36]. The present-day presence of Syrian refugees is in addition to the significant presence of Palestinian refugees living in Jordan which remains an "unresolved question" for the host-nation ([16], online). A 2022 survey conducted by 'Headway Jordan' and commissioned by the UNHCR, however, revealed that 95% of Jordanian locals were sympathetic towards refugees who fled conflict or persecution, with most survey participants stating that they are in favour of the inclusion of refugees in Jordanian national systems, such as health and education [39]. This attitude among locals is reflected in Jordan's refugee response since the outbreak of the Syrian civil war which has allowed Syrian refugees inclusion in critical areas such as education, healthcare, and lately, access to national COVID-19 health and vaccination programmes [36].

Nonetheless, the influx of Syrian asylum-seekers and refugees in the last decade continues to place significant pressure on the Jordan's pre-existing social, political, economic, and legal structures and institutions, thereby hindering Jordan's recovery [36]. During the third quarter of 2022, the World Bank documented a chronic employment crisis in Jordan, particularly among youth and women, due primarily to a lack of labour force expansion and a weak business environment [36]. Nonetheless, Jordan continues to receive assistance, and fiscal contributions and aid, from international alliances and donors. United Nations bodies, such as the UN High Commissioner for Refugees (UNHCR) continue to be particularly active in offering Jordan humanitarian assistance, and legal and security support, through the Jordanian Ministry of Interior for issues such as refugee registrations, and camp maintenance and coordination [32]. As well, the UN Children's Fund (UNICEF), works alongside the Jordanian institutions, such as the Ministry of Education, to support children's rights and development, through education, health and nutrition, and social protection [32]. This international support has greatly alleviated pressures within Jordan to allow greater response and action for refugee protections and opportunities.

1.2 Approach and Structure of the Book

The primary focus of this book is to highlight and explore the reasons for the ongoing endemic of child marriages among Syrian refugee children in Jordan. It does so cognisant that not only is the cohort vulnerable to forced marriage because they are children, but they are also vulnerable because they have been displaced and live in another state with unclear legal status and future prospects. Focused on the double-bind of vulnerability of child refugees, this book aims to contribute to the critical need to advance protections for refugee children against violent practices during displacement and resettlement, specifically, forced child marriage.

This chapter has conceptualised the 'age' of the Middle Eastern refugee. It introduced the nature of the Syrian conflict as the leading cause of the mass displacement of Syrian civilians within the last decade, and additionally, examined the nature of, and reasons for, Jordan's responses. Chapter 2 provides a critical literature-based discussion of the modern-day practice of child marriage and the concept of childhood vulnerability. Discussion regarding childhood vulnerability is further expanded and examined from a gendered perspective to consider the complex web of factors that inform the life of a girl bride. The chapter evaluates the physical, social, economic, and legal impacts of violence for young vulnerable refugee girls. The exacerbated vulnerabilities of children because of gendered practices like child marriage is further contextualised by examining Syrian refugee girls' experiences in Jordan.

Chapter 3 systematically analyses the contributions and shortcomings of international human rights instruments currently in place for the protection of refugees, generally, and refugee children, specifically. While there is a demonstrated commitment by the UN and its member states, including Jordan, to harmoniously create safe spaces for refugees, there appears to be a distinct discrepancy at the local and regional levels with regard to binding legal protections. Arguably, a state's failure to adhere to the instruments and conventions it ratifies, consequently demonstrates a failure on part of the UN and its role as a governing body to ensure the universal protection of all individuals, especially children. This chapter, thus, seeks to examine the legal-governance aspects of child and refugee protections against gender-based violence and forced marriages.

Chapter 4 critically examines the 'universality' of international human rights instruments through a dichotomous comparison of 'Western' and 'Arab' interpretations and application of international laws. It further critically examines the legislative and judicial system of the state of Jordan which is characterised by pluralist 'Western' and 'Arab' notions. Significantly, this chapter interrogates the implications of Jordan's legal pluralism for women and children's rights.

Lastly, this book seeks to explore the future of vulnerable child brides by examining child marriage as both an ongoing social and cultural practice affecting the lives of innumerable children worldwide, as well as, a legal violation of international human rights. While global, regional, and national attention and responses to ending forced child marriage are growing, important gaps in child marriage prevention remain. Within Chap. 5, child marriage is, thus, conceptualised as both an impediment to the realisation of universal rights for humans worldwide, as well as a motivation for the enforcement and coordination of human rights protections by the international community, especially for those most vulnerable and voiceless.

References

1. Akpinar P (2016) The limits of mediation in the Arab Spring: the case of Syria. Third World Q 36(12):2288–2303
2. Al Jazeera (2023) Twelve years on from the beginning of Syria's war. Al Jazeera. https://aje.io/rvidaa
3. Ali O (1997) The Kurds and the Lausanne peace negotiations, 1922–23. Middle Eastern Stud 33(3):521–534. http://www.jstor.org/stable/4283891
4. Aras B, Falk R (2015) Authoritarian 'geopolitics' of survival in the Arab Spring. Third World Q 36(2):322–336. Babar Z (2020) Human mobility in the Middle East. In: Babar Z (ed) Mobility and forced displacement in the Middle East. Oxford University Press, UK, 1–18
5. Bae CJ, Douka K, Petraglia MD (2017) On the origin of modern humans: Asian perspectives. Science 358(6368). https://doi.org/10.1126/science.aai9067
6. Bakewell O (2011) Conceptualising displacement and migration: processes, conditions, and categories. In: Koser K, Martin S (eds) The migration-displacement nexus: patterns, processes, and policies. Berghahn Books, USA, pp 14–28
7. Bloch, A. (2020). Reflections and directions for research in refugee studies. Ethnic and Racial Studies, 43(3) 436–459. https://doi.org/10.1080/01419870.2020.1677928
8. Cazabat C (2018) The ripple effect: economic impacts of internal displacement. Internal Displacement Monitoring Centre. https://www.internal-displacement.org/sites/default/files/inline-files/201810-literature-review-economic-impacts.pdf
9. Centre for Preventative Action (CPA) (2023) Global conflict tracker: conflict in Syria. Council on Foreign Affairs. https://www.cfr.org/global-conflict-tracker/conflict/conflict-syria
10. Chatty D, Finlayson B (eds) (2010) Dispossession and displacement: forced migration in the Middle East and North Africa. British Academy
11. Council on Foreign Relations (2023) The Kurds' long struggle with statelessness (1920–2022). Retrieved from: https://www.cfr.org/timeline/kurds-long-struggle-statelessness#:~:text=The%20Kurds%20are%20one%20of,marked%20by%20marginalization%20and%20persecution
12. Feller E (2005) Refugees are not migrants. Refugee Surv Q 24(4):27–35. http://www.jstor.org/stable/45054030
13. Flapan S (1987) The Palestinian exodus of 1948. J Palest Stud 16(4):3–26. https://doi.org/10.2307/2536718

14. Gelvin JL (2015) The Arab uprisings: what everyone needs to know, 2nd edn. Oxford University Press, New York
15. Griffiths M (2023) Briefing to the security council on the humanitarian situation in Syria, 29 June 2023. UN Office for the Coordination of Humanitarian Affairs. https://reliefweb.int/attachments/5c2d4b6e-cece-4b26-89af-c0aa35ca52ac/Martin%20Griffiths%2029%20June%202023-2.pdf
16. Kaya A (2023) Seeking asylum in the Middle East: lessons from the Syrian crisis. In: Triandafyllidou A (ed) Routledge handbook of immigration and refugee studies, 2nd edn. Routledge, New York, pp 396–404
17. Kinninmont J (2014) The Syria conflict and the geopolitics of the region. In: IEMed Mediterranean yearbook 2014. Insitut Europeu de la Mediterrania, Barcelona, Spain
18. Lageman T (2020) Remembering Mohamed Bouazizi: the man who sparked the Arab Spring. Al Jazeera. https://aje.io/7xwjx
19. Laub Z (2023) Syria's civil war: the descent into horror. Council on Foreign Relations. https://www.cfr.org/article/syrias-civil-war
20. Ma'oz M (2014) The Arab spring in Syria: domestic and regional developments. Dyn Asymmetric Conflict 7(1):47–57. https://doi.org/10.1080/17467586.2014.894249
21. Malkki L (1992) National geographic: the rooting of peoples and the territorialization of national identity among scholars and refugees. Cult Anthropol 7(1):24–44
22. Moghadam VM (2013) What is democracy? Promises and perils of the Arab Spring. Curr Sociol 61(4):393–408. https://doi.org/10.1177/0011392113479739
23. Olwan M, Shiyab A (2012) Forced migration of Syrians to Jordan: an exploratory study [Migration Policy Centre Research Report 2012/06]. European University Institute, Florence, Italy
24. Omer S (2023) 2023 Turkey and Syria earthquake: facts, FAQs, how to help. World Vision. https://www.worldvision.org/disaster-relief-news-stories/2023-turkey-and-syria-earthquake-faqs
25. Said EW (2000) Reflections on exile and other essays. Harvard University Press, Cambridge, USA
26. Shakir O (2023) 75 Years later, Israel blocking Palestinian refugees' return. Human Rights Watch. https://www.hrw.org/news/2023/05/15/75-years-later-israel-blocking-palestinian-refugees-return
27. Shami S (1996) Transnationalism and refugee studies: rethinking forced migration and identity in the Middle East. J Refug Stud 9(1):3–26
28. Sorenson DS (2016) Syria in ruins: the dynamics of the Syrian Civil war. Praeger, Santa Barbara
29. Syrian Observatory for Human Rights (SOHR) (2023) Syrian revolution 12 years on. Retrieved from: https://www.syriahr.com/en/291981/
30. Tarabay J (2018) For many Syrians, the story of the war began with graffiti in Dara'a. CNN. https://www.cnn.com/2018/03/15/middleeast/daraa-syria-seven-years-on-intl
31. Turner, V. (1967). The Forest of Symbols. Aspects of Ndembu Ritual. Ithaca, N.Y.: Cornell University Press
32. United Nations (UN) Jordan (2023) 2022 UN Country annual results report: Jordan. https://shorturl.at/gzL59
33. United Nations Children's Fund (UNICEF) (2023) Syrian crisis. Retrieved from: https://www.unicef.org/emergencies/syrian-crisis
34. United Nations High Commissioner for Refugees (UNHCR) (2022a) Middle East and North Africa. Retrieved from: https://reporting.unhcr.org/globalreport/middle-east-and-north-africa
35. United Nations High Commissioner for Refugees (UNHCR) (2022b) Ukraine, other conflicts push forcibly displaced total over 100 million for first time. Retrieved from: https://www.unrefugees.org/news/unhcr-ukraine-other-conflicts-push-forcibly-displaced-total-over-100-million-for-first-time/
36. United Nations High Commissioner for Refugees (UNHCR) (2022c) Annual results report 2022: Jordan. https://reporting.unhcr.org/files/2023-06/MENA%20-%20Jordan.pdf

37. United Nations High Commissioner for Refugees (UNHCR) (2023a) Global trends: forced displacement in 2022. https://www.unhcr.org/global-trends-report-2022
38. United Nations High Commissioner for Refugees (UNHCR) (2023b) Syrian refugees. https://www.unicef.org/media/131831/file/2023-HAC-Syrian-Refugees.pdf
39. United Nations High Commissioner for Refugees (UNHCR) (2023c) UNHCR survey: 95% of Jordanians feel sympathy with refugees. Retrieved from https://www.unhcr.org/jo/23181-unhcr-survey-95-of-jordanians-feel-sympathy-with-refugees.html
40. United Nations (2023) Security Council: 12 years of war, leaves 70 per cent of Syrians needing aid. UN News. https://news.un.org/en/story/2023/01/1132837
41. Weil S (2002) The need for roots: prelude to a declaration of duties towards mankind. Routledge, London
42. World Vision (2023) Syrian refugee crisis: facts, FAQs, and how to help. Retrieved from: https://www.worldvision.org/refugees-news-stories/syrian-refugee-crisis-facts
43. Zetter R (1988) Refugees and refugee studies a label and an agenda. J Refug Stud 1(1):1–6

Chapter 2
Understanding Child Marriage: Law and Practice

Child marriage is a global problem [28]. But what is it? 'Child marriage' is a term used to objectively refer to a practice involving the "legal or customary union between two people, of whom one or both spouses are below the age of 18 years" ([91], p. 11). It is often synonymously referred to as 'early' or 'forced' marriage. In reality, the practice of child marriage is a fundamental violation of human rights (UNICEF [77]). In 2023, it was estimated that around 640 million girls and women alive today were married before their 18th birthday [78]—that is 21% of girls, worldwide [95]. This statistic equates to 12 million girls each year, or 22 girls every minute, who are forcibly married before the age of 18 [95]. Even though child marriage is an internationally condemned human rights violation, child marriage remains a prevalent ongoing issue that occurs around the world.

From a sociolegal perspective, the issue of child marriage is a violation of international human rights on the basis of two core legally binding elements that are addressed in several key international human rights instruments: the first being 'age' and the second being 'consent'. In the first instance regarding age, the widely accepted definition of a 'child' within international law is based in accordance with Article 1 of the 1989 UN *Convention of the Rights of the Child* (hereafter 'CRC'). For the purposes of the Convention, a child is defined as "any human being below the age of eighteen years unless under the law applicable to the child, majority is attained earlier" ([85], p. 2). In the second instance, the concept 'consent' largely forms the basis of the definitional practice of 'marriage' within international law. Article 16 of the Universal Declaration of Human Rights (UDHR), for example, states that marriage shall only be entered into by "men and women of full age who have the right to marry" with the "… free and full consent of the intending spouses" [84]. The notion of 'consent' is further emphasised within Article 1 of the 1962 UN Convention on Consent to Marriage, Minimum Age for Marriage and Registration of Marriages, which states that "no marriage shall be legally entered into without the full and free consent of both parties" ([83], p. 1). Based on the view that children are not of 'full

S. Strungaru, *The Hidden Child Brides of the Syrian Civil War*,
SpringerBriefs in Law, https://doi.org/10.1007/978-981-97-2159-7_2

age', they are, therefore, deemed unable to personally express their free and full informed consent to enter marriage (UNFPA & UNICEF 2020; [14]).

There is, however, no universal statutory provision within international law that stipulates a consensual minimum age for marriage (UNFPA & UNICEF 2020). For international non-governmental organisation ([16], p. 1), a 'key pillar' to ending child marriages around the world is instituting a global "supportive legal framework which sets the age of marriage for girls and boys at 18 without exceptions" within domestic laws. While many countries have set 18 as the minimum legal age of consent to marriage without exceptions, in line with international human rights standards, this is often not enforced by authorities. As a result, child marriage is often authorised with parental and national judicial consent [16]. According to organisations such as the UN Population Fund and UN Children's Fund (2020), and [16], enforcing laws that set a minimum age of marriage to 18 institutes an objective standard of maturity worldwide that prevents discrimination. A minimum age is critical in safeguarding children from marriage when they lack both the legal rights of an adult, as well as, the physical, mental, and emotional maturity to "reach their full potential" (UNFPA & UNICEF 2020, p. 1).

While a clear and consistent legislation that establishes a minimum of age for marriage is an important part of addressing and ending child marriage, equal attention must be placed on sociocultural factors contributing to this practice (UNFPA & UNICEF 2020; [16]). Sociocultural strategies and tools for preventing child marriage include, for example, implementing a 'norm change approach' to the problem whereby social group norms and perceptions that perpetrate the practice of child marriage are identified and reconceptualised. In the case of child marriage, changes to normative perceptions about the practice may include providing valid alternatives to marriage, such as, "meaningful educational and employment opportunities" targeted equally to both girls and boys ([16], p. 1). According to Cislaghi et al. [13], norm change largely occurs in people's 'reference groups', that is, networks of shared norms and beliefs. These networks consist mainly of social or formal institutions and authority figures, such as the family, schools, places of worship, or governments, as well as, social groups with a shared membership, such as, members of interest or hobby groups, school peers, or workplace colleagues.

Notably, however, child marriages are typically arranged by a child's parents [70]. Two key drivers contributing to ongoing cases of child marriage worldwide are 'poverty and insecurity', and 'tradition'. With regard to the former, many parents consider marriage the most necessary means of securing a future for their daughter, especially in contexts of social instability or fragility [37]. Forced marriages arranged by parents often disproportionately affect girls (than boys) who are forced to marry a man they usually only meet after the wedding ceremony occurs, and who is also typically much older than the child bride [70]. Girls are also often viewed as 'economic burdens' or 'commodities' [37]. In this way, forced child marriage is often approved in order for the girl and her family to gain financial security, and to reduce the perceived burden that children place on poor families.

In the second instance, child marriage often occurs because of social and cultural norms, and religious or customary traditions [47]. Baghdassarian [8] and An-Na'im

[5] argue that an often overlooked yet significant cultural factor contributing to child marriage practices involves the notion of age. In many social and cultural contexts, age is a determinant of one's sexual 'purity', and therefore, 'desirability'. In other words, the younger a girl is, the 'purer' she is considered. This is particularly prevalent among communities where patriarchal values and gender norms are dominant, and a girl's virginity is highly valued [51]. In these communities, gendered social norms often "aim to control female sexuality" ([20], online). As such, child marriage is often supported as "the only legitimate context of sexual activity for girls", and subsequent means of "protection against potential disgrace if girls circumvent those norms" ([51], p. 15). Furthermore, the practice of marriage typically signifies a child's 'coming of age' into adulthood. Here, child marriage assumes the expectation that children will adopt the responsibility of primary caregiver within the household [68].

More often than not, significant age gaps between the child bride and her spouse, typical among cases of child marriage, assumes a relationship of disproportionate power relations where the child bride typically becomes financially and socially dependent solely on their spouse. This dependency thereby increases the child's vulnerability to domestic violence and abuse [70]. This book notes the need to consider 'cohabitation' within conceptualisations of marriage, because it "raises the same human rights concerns" (UNICEF 2023; see also [14]). Cohabitation refers to when a child under the age of eighteen lives together with a usually older partner 'in union', as if married (UNICEF 2023). According to UNICEF (2023), the informality of cohabitation presents additional concerns that may make children "vulnerable in different ways than those who are formally married", including (but not limited to), a child's lack of inheritance, citizenship, and social recognition (UNICEF 2023). The conceptualisation of cohabitation, therefore, expands upon traditional understandings of customary laws and local norms regarding marriage, and provides a more comprehensive picture of the nature and extent of relationships and unions involving children around the world [14].

Under international human rights law, the practice of child marriage (including cohabitation) is consistent with understandings of bonded labour and enslavement. This is because the practice is a clear violation of a child's right to live their lives to their fullest potential and to express their views regarding decisions that will shape the entire course of their lives (UNFPA 2012). The practice denies children the right to be free from all forms of discrimination, degrading treatment, and gender inequality norms. According to de Silva-de-Alwis ([98], p. i) child marriage "violates a panoply of interconnected rights" as stipulated in various UN instruments including

> … the right to equality on grounds of sex and age, the right to marry and start a family, the right to life, the right to the highest attainable standard of health, the right to education and development, and the right to be free from slavery.

As noted above, child marriage occurs due to a complex web of factors including, but not limited to, "poverty, weak legislative frameworks and enforcement, harmful traditional practices, gender discrimination, and lack of alternative opportunities for girls (especially education)" ([45], p. 17). At its foundation, child marriage is an outcome of interrelated and cumulative discriminatory gender-based social norms, beliefs, and perceptions, mediated by "broader sociocultural (including ideational/religious), political, and economic contexts" ([25], p. 31). Not surprisingly, the consequences of abruptly bringing a child's childhood and adolescence to an "unnatural end" through forced marriage also has long-term detrimental effects on their physical, emotional, and mental health (UNFPA 2012, p. 11). Additionally, when children, particularly girls, are forced to marry, they are often denied their rights to development and childhood, especially access to healthcare and education, thereby consequently exacerbating childhood vulnerability, as will be examined in this chapter (UNFPA & UNICEF 2020).

The practice of child marriage thus severely impedes upon progressive international human rights standards that "recognise the right of women and girls to live free from physical, mental and sexual violence" ([22], online). Any enforcement of international laws, or the development of national legislation, therefore, needs to understand the reasons for child marriage as constituting social, cultural, economic, and religious factors, as well norms and attitudes related to family status and regional understandings. More so, changes to child marriage practices and its legal status and recourse, needs to be contextualised within the 'cultural biases' some states have towards existing international human rights law [5]—a point returned to later in this book.

2.1 The Vulnerable Child, Rights and Discourse

This discussion has highlighted that children who are forced into marriage face a plethora of vulnerabilities that cause long-term impacts to a child's livelihood and wellbeing. On this basis, it can be reasonably ascertained that the child bride is vulnerable. More broadly, children in general are positioned as the most vulnerable members of society [61]. The notion of the vulnerable child is prevalent in legal frameworks and responses to childhood, and portrayals within the media [21]. But what does it mean to be vulnerable? According to Mackenzie et al. [39] and Herring [21], vulnerability is a condition of human life. Mackenzie et al. [39] describe human vulnerability in three main ways: physically, socially, and socio-politically. As physical beings, humans are vulnerable to physical illness, injury, and death. This condition of vulnerability is often the most orthodox understanding of the concept which is derived from the Latin word 'vulnus', meaning 'wound' [39]. Secondly, as social beings, humans are susceptible to emotional and psychological vulnerability from exposure to situations, such as, loss and grief, neglect and abuse, and rejection and humiliation. Lastly, as socio-political beings, humans are vulnerable to political violence, abuse of their rights, exploitation, and oppression [39]. Accordingly, these states of vulnerability emphasise the social and relational nature of a person or group's susceptibility to harm. In other words, the state of being vulnerable is often largely attributed to the "contingent susceptibility of persons to specific kinds of harm or threat by others" (p. 6). The view that all human life is conditioned by vulnerability, however, does not consider the notion that certain groups of individuals, such as children, are fundamentally more vulnerable than others. This book considers Schroeder and Gefenas' [63] 'elements' approach to vulnerability to argue that particularly vulnerable groups are both susceptible to exposure to the possibility of harm or danger (the 'external' element, as well as, lack the ability or capacity, power, or control to protect themselves (the 'internal' element [39, 63]. It is this 'internal' element which this book considers pertinent to childhood vulnerability, particularly with regard to refugee children.

In this way, the notion of childhood vulnerability suggests that children are a specific group of social and emotional beings unequally predisposed to, or at greater risk of, harm from external conditions and structures [6]. Referring to Mackenzie et al. [39] triadic definition of vulnerability (physical, emotional, and socio-political) presented earlier, childhood vulnerability may be conceptualised, as follows: firstly, due to the physical stature of a child which is generally small in size vis-à-vis an adult body, children are perceived as considerably weaker in their physical abilities, and are, thus, physically vulnerable. The physiology of a child is also at higher risk of exposure to, and absorption of, a higher percentage of pollutants that can compromise their immune systems [61]. Secondly, a child's emotional vulnerability suggests that they characteristically lack emotional maturity and self-control, and are often less socially skilled to comprehend, respond to, or acknowledge complex interactions and emotions [21]. Lastly, socio-political childhood vulnerability refers to unequal power relations between adults and children. In addition to physical and emotional immaturity, children also largely lack a 'public voice' [61], and may, thus, be subordinated by adults who may manipulate them into harm for their own interests [21, 55].

A child is almost entirely and 'inevitably dependent' upon their family members or adult caregivers—a relationship essential for both surviving and flourishing [32, 38]. Research shows that children identify three primary factors as providing them with a sense of safety and positive well-being: "being protected by parents, having a personal safe place, and having trusted people in their lives" (Fattore et al. [15], cited in [10], p. 101). The home and family are, thus, seen as key determinants of childhood experiences that provide children with an environment that likely reduces their vulnerability. Globally, however, perpetrators of violence against children are usually individuals the child knows, or those who are close to the child's family, typically parents, relatives, spouses of child brides, or teachers. Sadly, parental violence against children is one of the most common forms of violence experienced by children which is often perpetrated because of tradition, culture, religion, or even superstition [27].

Furthermore, in their discussion of vulnerability, Mackenzie et al. [39], suggest two main (although not categorically distinct) sources of vulnerability—inherent and situational. Inherent vulnerability is defined by Mackenzie et al. ([39], p. 7) as sources of vulnerability that are "intrinsic to the human condition", based largely on an individual's corporeality and dependence on others. According to Mackenzie et al. [39], symptoms of 'inherent' vulnerability, such as, hunger, thirst, physical and/or emotional harm, and social isolation, vary according to specific factors, such as, age, gender, and health conditions or disabilities. Inherent vulnerabilities also reflect, "to a greater or lesser extent features of the environment in which individuals are born and raised and live", and one's capacity or resilience to cope within a given environment (p. 8). For example, health status may reflect a person's vulnerability to socioeconomic factors. 'Situational vulnerability' refers to vulnerability that is context specific, it is "caused or exacerbated by the personal, social, political, economic, or environmental situations" of individuals and social groups (p. 7). Exposure to situational vulnerability can be either enduring, intermittent, or short term.

Vulnerability is particularly exacerbated when children live in poverty, are separated from their families, displaced from their homes, live in conflict zones, and/or have limited access to education. Here, wealth or a lack thereof, in this regard, is necessarily seen as one of the main factors of socially determined childhood vulnerability as children are deemed unable to fully comprehend their situation and its severity and are, therefore, likely to be manipulated into violence and dangerous situations, such as, armed recruitment, and sexual exploitation and abuse [6]. For refugee children, particularly girls who have been forced into marriage, the factors exacerbating their vulnerability may be characterised as both inherent and situational. As will be discussed further within this chapter, 'situational vulnerability' is particularly relevant with relation to child marriage in the Middle Eastern context.

Presently, millions of children worldwide have experienced or continue to experience violence, exploitation, and discrimination, including exclusion from decision-making processes contrary to their human rights [36]. In 2022, the World Health Organisation estimated that up to 1 billion children aged between 2 and 17 years, have experienced violence—either physical, emotional, sexual, or neglect [93]. In 2021, UNICEF [74] further estimated that 3 in 4 children (around 300 million) between the ages of 2 and 4 are regularly subjected to violent discipline by their caregivers, according to the UNICEF [74]; however, about 9% of children live in countries where legal protection from corporal punishment is prohibited. For UNICEF ([74], p. 1), "violence against children is a pervasive human rights violation…usually hidden from public view".

Moreover, a child's capabilities and the extent of their vulnerability or, more appropriately, the nature and levels of risks against children present in a given environment, is highly contextual. In other words, various societies and cultures construct different assumptions of 'childhood' and vulnerability that inform how children should be treated and what they are deemed competent to achieve [34]. In many states in the Global South, for example, children are often viewed as an "economic investment with a return" that often "overshadows various other aspects of the value of the child" ([52], pp. 612–3). In this regard, many countries in the Global South often deem it acceptable for children to hold high levels of social and economic responsibilities all while their "rights to negotiate those contributions, or to exercise autonomous choices are likely restricted" ([34], p. 31). One such example of this is child marriage. UNICEF [77] indicates that child marriage rates are highest in West and Central Africa, with nearly 4 in 10 young women married before the age of 18, followed by Eastern and Southern Africa, South Asia, and Latin America and

Caribbean. In comparison, in most Western societies and states in the Global North, while there is a higher value on civil and political liberties and autonomy, children are mostly absent from opportunities for participation in the exercise of responsibilities and decision-making [34]. This is largely because within these economically advanced Western societies, children are often socially and economically dependent on their caregivers, and perceived as requiring a constant need for protection [34]. One such example, is the prevailing assumption in the Global North that school is more appropriate for childhood development than work. This Western construction of childhood has largely informed, and continues to increasingly dominate, the construction of international children's rights agendas and frameworks. Article 3.1 of the 1973 International Labour Organisation (ILO) *Minimum Age Convention (No. 138)*, for example, stipulates "the minimum age for admission to any type of employment or work which by its nature or the circumstances in which it is carried out is likely to jeopardise the health, safety or morals of young persons shall not be less than 18 years [26]". The ratification of this convention was recently emphasised during the 2023 UN World Day Against Child Labour, the theme of which was 'Social Justice for All. End Child Labour'.

The common practice of citing 'vulnerability' with 'childhood', particularly in Western societies, has played a significant role in the ways childhood has been constructed, and how academic, medical, and legal discourses have understood and responded to children, their needs, and rights [21]. Notably, sociolegal debates have, on the other hand, continued to question whether children's vulnerability should "provide the basis for special human rights for children" ([67], p. 156). 'Rights', in this context, are understood as both an obligation to be protected, and an obligation to not harm others [67]. For some commentators, children's lack of capacity to understand and exercise these rights, in addition to their dependence on adults, are used as reasons for precluding children from holding rights [67]. For proponents of this theory, such as Harry Bighouse, the "capacity to exercise rights" is, therefore, "a prerequisite to the entitlement to rights" ([67], p. 158). Archard ([7], cited in [21], p. 243) takes this argument further by asserting that in "granting fundamental liberties to a child before [s]/he possesses the capacities to be the guardian of [their] own life" is "cruel". While children's perceived physical immaturity, relative inexperience, and lack of knowledge, "render them vulnerable and necessitate specific protections", contra-arguments for children's rights are that children's capabilities are increasingly underestimated by adults under the guise of 'vulnerability' [34], inevitably, a child becomes disassociated "from decision-making opportunities in accordance with their evolving capabilities" ([34], p. 31). As a result of these ongoing debates, childhood vulnerability has become a social and political issue that only further reinforce power inequalities between adults and children, and entrench children's vulnerabilities [6], as Schroeder and Gefenas' [63] boldly assert, "it doesn't need an academic to say what vulnerability is…we can all see it, much more often than we care to". For this reason, this book affirms the position taken by Herring [21], that children are in fact vulnerable, and that the law is rightfully placed to regard children as such.

Significantly, the vulnerable status of children plays a critical role within international children's rights laws in informing and implementing the protection of the special interests of children within key international treaties and conventions. The main international treaty on children's rights is the *Convention on the Rights of the Child* (CRC) which was adopted in 1989. It is the most widely ratified human rights treaty in the world. The preamble to the CRC [79] affords specific consideration to the vulnerable nature of the child by recalling the UN's proclamation that "childhood is entitled to special care and assistance", as noted within preceding international instruments, such as, the 1948 UDHR; the 1924 *Geneva Declaration of the Rights of the Child*; the 1959 *Declaration of the Rights of the Child*; as well as, within the *International Covenant on Civil and Political Rights* (in particular in articles 23 and 24), and the *International Covenant on Economic, Social and Cultural Rights* (in particular in article 10). The CRC [79] encompasses a range of civil, political, social, and cultural rights for the child, including, but not limited to, the right of all children to enjoy all the rights set forth in the CRC without discrimination of any kind (Article 2.1); respect for the best interests of the child as a primary consideration (Article 3.1); the right to survival and development (Article 6.2); and the right of all children to express their views freely on all matters affecting them (Article 12.1).

2.1.1 Gendered Child Vulnerability and Inequality

While significant progress continues to be made globally in addressing the rights of children collectively as a social group, it is impractical to conceptualise all children as a single homogenous group. Individual experiences of childhood vulnerability are likely to be highly differentiated and effected by a range of factors, such as, gender, class, and/or ethnicity that may significantly heighten a child's inequality [6, 21] Gender, for example, remains one of the main factors that significantly impact the assumptions and limitations children are likely to encounter, particularly girls [34]. Gendered dimensions of childhood vulnerability consider the physical, social, economic, and political impacts of gendered discrimination and violence in structural, institutional, and customary settings. Worldwide, millions of girls are frequently denied their access to resources, opportunities, and power and agency, which inevitably oppresses and limits their personal and professional choices, denies them their basic human rights, and often leads to gender-based violence being perpetrated against them [76].

Gendered vulnerability has also been appropriately conceptualised within international law as the 'feminisation of poverty'. Coined in the 1970s and later officially utilised by the UN during the 1995 'Beijing Platform for Action', the 'feminisation of poverty' is a term used to refer to the phenomenon in which women and children are disproportionately impacted by poverty, and more likely than men to live below the poverty line [11]. This concept has profoundly contributed to the acknowledgment that there is, in fact, a "gender dimension to poverty" [81]. The concept is instrumental in capturing the reality of gendered vulnerability in discourses whereby girls and women exist as subjects of a dual labour market of paid and unpaid labour [57]. Here, women and girls around the world are significantly denied access to "critical resources such as credit, land and inheritance", "being unrewarded and unrecognised for their labour", "lacking sufficient access to health care and support services, and education", as well as being excluded in opportunities to participate in decision-making at home and in the community [81].

Girls are particularly vulnerable because their individual agency and freedom to make their own life choices is often largely circumscribed and dictated by individuals, institutions, and structures in their life, including parents and family members, school, religion, government, and judicial systems [59]. These powerful actors not only individually influence a girl's freedom and the dimensions of her life but create discriminatory social norms regarding girls' roles in society respective to that of boys [59]. Characteristically, these gendered social norms become entrenched within society and are inevitably internalised by females themselves, "reducing their sense of agency" from a young age and making them less likely to participate in social, economic, or political life, and likely hesitant to challenge discrimination ([59], p. 2). In 2022, UNICEF published a report illustrating concerning statistics about the state of gendered inequality around the world. According to the report almost twice as many adolescent girls (1 in 4) than boys (1 in 10) worldwide are not receiving any forms of education or training. In least developed countries, girls are twice as likely as boys to spend 21 h or more a week on household chores [76].

A girl's vulnerability and exposure to gender discrimination, and gendered norms and practices, also substantiates a greater probability of girls experiencing significantly higher rates of physical, sexual, and emotional violence against them than boys may experience [71]. The onset of puberty in particular makes girls acutely vulnerable to sexual violence [70]. In 2022, it was estimated that around 13 million girls (1 in 20) worldwide have experienced forced, or non-consensual, sex [76]. According to data from 30 countries, only 1% of girl victims of forced sex have sought professional help [65]. Research suggests that the objectification and sexualisation of girls are key contributors to sexual violence being perpetrated against them [31, 65]. As Swift and Gould [65] note, there tends to be a universal message transmitted by media texts that "that girls should be pretty, not powerful, noticed, not respected". This is particularly relevant with regard to girls' increased exposure to social media platforms where there is a growing online 'influencer' culture. Increased exposure to normative discourse is not only incredibly harmful for girls and their development, but to cultures at large [65].

Furthermore, in many cultures, notions of puberty or 'coming of age' often carry the expectation for girls to assume gender roles typically associated with 'womanhood', such as, wives and mothers [71]. As presented earlier within this chapter, the expectation of a girl to assume mature (adult) responsibilities is largely seen in societies in the Global South, particularly where high incidences of child marriage are reported. This concept is, however, not unique to the Global South. While there is a general trend toward increased female participation in work and education, and a general social polarisation of motherhood in Western societies, Wyn and White ([96], p. 59) remind us how education systems in Western societies in the 1950s conditioned young women to construct 'self-determining' identities by thinking of themselves "first and foremost as sexed individuals",this strategically ensured that part of the process of "finding their 'true' identity" girls would "'naturally' choose to become wives and mothers" (p. 59). Today, 15% of young women aged 20 to 24 years around the world became mothers before the 18 [76].

Although both boys and girls face the risk of being married, the vast majority of victims of child marriage worldwide are girls [82]. Along with other harmful practices, such as, female genital mutilation, child marriage is considered a practice of gender-based violence [19]. Practices of gender-based violence occurs largely because of social and cultural attitudes often guised within traditional religious discourse, together with institutional and legal approaches, that discriminate and disempower girls and women [25, 64]. For Kamal et al. ([29], p. 21), harmful gender-based violence practices against girls continues to be fuelled by "a dangerous combination of entrenched poverty and customs deeply embedded in patriarchal societies". The sexualisation of girls, is typically enforced by the restrictions placed upon girls, their low status in society and within their families, as well as, the propensity of men and boys to hold and exert power. These factors exacerbate their exposure to harmful practices such as female genital mutilation and child marriage, "both of which are direct manifestations of gender inequality" ([71], p. 1). Here, gender inequality may not only contribute to the prevalence of violence but also to its 'acceptability', to the extent that gender-based violent practices, such as, female genital mutilation and child marriage may not even be recognised as human rights infringements in a given society, nor will girls themselves consider these violations as violence or abuse against them [71]. These cases of normative sexual victimisation are what makes girls so vulnerable.

For societies where child marriage is sanctioned and where a culture of male dominance pervades, intimate partner violence may, thus, be perceived as an "ordinary component of interpersonal dynamics between the sexes, particularly in the context of marriage or other formal unions" ([71], p. 5). According to UNICEF [76], nearly 1 in 4 girls who are, or have been, married or in informal unions have experienced physical and/or intimate partner violence at least once in their lifetime. Girls will not only carry a set of 'normalised' expectations of violence with them into a marriage ([71], p. 15), but the practice will consequently remain "hidden by a strong culture of silence" ([33], 3). This pervasive 'culture' of silence, however, exceeds the notion that gender-based violence is a practice that is merely under- or entirely unreported. Rather, it suggests, that girls who are victim of gender-based violence will often be blamed for the violations, coerced into keeping abuse secret, and often stigmatised and marginalised should they speak of violations against them [49]. The concept of 'voicelessness', in this regard, is not so much an innate predisposition associated with vulnerability denoting a limitation to speak or express an opinion. In the case of child brides, 'voicelessness' refers to a state of being "deliberately silenced or…preferably unheard" that renders an "all-encompassing and yet specifically targeted … assault on vulnerable, fragile sections of society" ([56], online).

Child brides who are forced to marry—oftentimes to significantly older men—are not only at greater risk of intimate partner violence but are also at greater risk of adverse physical and mental health, and psychosocial outcomes that characteristically condemn a girl to a life of long-term complications, or may even cause premature death [45]. According to the World Health Organisation (WHO) ([94], online), "interpersonal violence is among the leading causes of death in adolescents and young people globally". The consequences of child marriage also place girls at high risk of sexually transmitted diseases, and complications during pregnancy or labour (UNFPA & UNICEF 2020; [75]). Injury and complications during intercourse, pregnancy, and/or childbirth is reported as one of the leading causes of death for girls aged 15—19 years globally due to the underdeveloped physiology of a girl's pelvic structure and birth canal [22, 94]. Globally, it is estimated that more than 22,000 girls die annually from pregnancy and childbirth [60]. The marginalisation of women and girls in society and their inability to control their fertility disempowers girls to a life of uncertainty, fear, and subordination, thereby rendering them a particularly vulnerable cohort [54, 62].

Girls who are victim to rape and intimate partner violence during their "formative stage of psychological development", while also facing emotional abuse and discrimination from her family, and her husband and his family respectively, can also have especially devastating mental health consequences on young girls which lead to increased risk of depression and self-harm [1, 94]. These effects and traumas can even be transmitted inter-generationally, in other words, children who witness violence in their childhood are twice as likely to perpetuate violence as adults" ([25], p. 39).

As presented, a girl's abrupt 'transition' into womanhood when forced into marriage is based on patriarchal norms and constructions of identity and sexuality that aim to reinforce unequal societal power relations that position masculine and feminine genders in diametric opposition to one another. As such, girls' vulnerability is not only characterised by their lack of understanding or preparedness in relation to the responsibilities and complexities associated with the roles of being a wife and mother [71]. Rather, vulnerability is associated with the negative consequences of being forced into gendered roles at such a young age. Inhibiting childhood experiences and development before the age of 18 results in a girl becoming isolated from important support networks, institutions, and services, which thereby often consequently deprive child brides the opportunity of completing their education, developing skills, and pursuing employment after they have been forced to marry (UNFPA & UNICEF 2020; [70]). While poverty is a key cause of child marriage (as previously noted), it is also a consequence of the practice [75].

2.2 Contextualising Child Marriages: The Region, Reasons, and Impacts

In Middle Eastern and North African contexts, governance structures and legal systems are based largely on culture and traditions "explicitly informed by Islam" ([25], p. 31). Within these predominantly Islamic communities, traditional kinship and religious networks markedly institutionalise discriminatory gender roles and different rights for men and women in both public and private spheres [25]. Within predominantly Islamic Arab states, patriarchal attitudes reflect the view that men are dominant figures within societal institutions, particularly in the family, and that women are inevitably subordinate and subservient to men. Gendered stereotypes are also socialised in children from a young age, for example, that boys are 'strong', 'aggressive' and 'competitive', whereas girls are 'weak', 'passive' and 'emotional' [18]. These patriarchal views are reflected in conservative gender roles children are expected to resume, such as, for girls to get married, and stay home and raise children [18]. In cases where an adult male is absent from within a family, it is often typical for the first-born male child to resume the status as 'head' of the household.

Gender roles and norms that place women and girls in subordinate roles to men, consequently, limits women's agency, "restricts their mobility and ability to participate in political or civil society", and, further, renders them voiceless in negotiating critical aspects to their livelihoods, and quite often, "the terms of marriage, divorce, citizenship or inheritance" ([25], p. 31). Subordination, furthermore, entrenches "harmful practices that are linked to women's value and fears around their sexual security" ([45], p. 22). In these contexts, the practice of child marriage is, thus, an often "unquestioned component of the social fabric" reflecting embedded patriarchal gender relations ([45], p. 22). Patriarchal attitudes toward women and girls' unequal place and roles in society, as reflected in both legal and discrimination by political and religious leadership, illustrates the dire need for "investment in social services, including education, which then may influence how child marriage is understood and practiced" ([25], p. 31). A lack of action against discriminatory laws and practices that heighten girls' vulnerability and impede upon gender equality progress and achievement, ultimately "condemns girls to a life of poverty" ([54], p. 7).

As touched upon earlier, child marriage further accentuates both a girl's powerlessness to refuse sex, and her vulnerability in the presence of usually older and sexually experienced men. Although most countries in the Middle East and North Africa region are signatories to the UN's Convention on the Elimination of All Forms of Discrimination Against Women (CEDAW) that was adopted in 1979, gender-based violence in its various, albeit disturbing, forms such as intimate or non-partner violence, female genital mutilation, and 'femicide'—that is, 'honour'-related murders of women and girls by men—remains a prevalent "though often invisible threat" ([25], p. 39, [92]). 'Femicides', in particular, conceptually differ to other forms of intentional murders because they are specifically based on either direct or indirect gender-related motivations [92]; that is, they involve, according to the 2015 report of the UN Secretary-General, "the intentional murder of women and girls because of their gender" ([87], p. 2). The perpetration of 'honour' killings not only presently remains prevalent within the Middle East and North Africa, but is, alarmingly, even accepted within many states [9]. In Egypt, for example, "62% of men and 49% of women agree with the practice, as do 32% of men and 12% of women in Morocco, and 26% and 8% in Lebanon" ([9], online). As a result of the detrimental gendered inequalities within institutions and systems, sentencing for perpetrators of gender-based violence continues to often be lenient [9]. Article 340(1) of the Jordanian Penal Code [43] is often cited by human rights organisations, for example, as providing legal justification for femicide in cases of 'adultery' whereby the perpetrator "shall benefit from a mitigation excuse".

Furthermore, rape and sexual assault are frequently employed as weapons of war in crisis zones, making females particularly vulnerable [69]. Sometimes, the source of a girl's exploitation and abuse may even be inflicted by trusted persons, such as, security personnel, charged with the duty to protect and offer children safety [69]. This has been seen among displaced Syrians who have been affected by conflict and displaced from their home country to neighbouring states [25]. For displaced families, marriage in times of uncertainty is often thought of as a way for them to protect their daughters against the cycle of poverty and potential sexual exploitation, including protection from rape in conflict settings, including within refugee camps [46]. These contexts thereby unfortunately exacerbate girls' vulnerability and voicelessness.

Observably, children within vulnerable environments, such as those affected by conflict and disaster, will necessarily lack the capacity and resources to report and testify against abuse perpetrated to them. As well, grassroots communities within vulnerable environments are often seen to also be limited in their capacity to influence or campaign stronger child-protection policies and laws. As a result, vulnerable communities and states with weak judicial frameworks or patriarchal governance structures, as widely seen across Middle East and North Africa, rely on, and default to, customary laws, practices, and protection networks, thereby inevitably facilitating the continuity of harmful practices such as child marriage [45]. In states including Syria, Algeria, Bahrain, Iraq, Kuwait, and Libya, for example, perpetrators of rape or assault are still exonerated if they marry the woman or child victim [9]. The 2010 case of 13-year-old Yemeni girl, Ilham Mahdi Al-Assi, who died due to severe haemorrhaging after a rupture to her sex organs after being forced to marry, remains a "flagrant example" of the disturbing reality of intimate partner violence and its intersection with discriminatory gender-based customs and traditions ([66], online). More than a decade following Al-Assi's death, Hunersen et al. [23] note that Yemen has still not set a minimum age for marriage, despite Yemen ratifying the Convention on the Rights of the Child (CRC) and acceding to the Convention on the Elimination of All Forms of Discrimination Against Women (CEDAW) which sets the minimum age of marriage at 18 and mandates the free and full consent to marriage, respectively.

Marginalised women and girls, including migrant domestic workers and forcibly displaced persons, are especially vulnerable to gender-based non-partner violence [9]. In Jordan, for example, 29% of Syrian refugee women reportedly experienced physical assault, and 28% experienced psychological abuse [9]. Where children are vulnerable, refugee children are even more so. For refugee children, the unfamiliar becomes a standard, especially within liminal spaces such as refugee camps, where the uncertainty of safety becomes a given [4]. The state of a child's vulnerability is, thus, compounded in situations of poverty, and forced migration and displacement, particularly within refugee camps which, according to Alsaud ([4], p. 228) are "not intended to serve" the best interests of the child.

The principle of the 'best interests of the child', as referred to by Alsaud [4], is an internationally recognised obligation, per Article 3.1 of the UN CRC, for parties and states to "give the child the right to have his or her best interests assessed and taken into account as a the primary consideration in all actions or decisions that concern him or her, both in the public and private sphere" ([80], p. 3). Despite the internationally-recognised need to prioritise children's rights, at the end of 2021, UN Assistant-Secretary-General for Human Rights, Ilze Brands Kehris, stated that more than 450 million children, or one in six, were living in a conflict zone—the highest number documented in 20 years [30]. These rates not only illustrate the magnitude of children's vulnerability but stress the dire and time-critical need for immediate preventative action and aid. Child refugees who have been displaced from their homes as the result of war are at risk of poverty, starvation, and disease due to a lack of access to shelter and warmth, nutritional food, education, and healthcare [48]. Displaced children are also vulnerable to emotional trauma, stress, fear, and confinement [48].

Necessarily, UN Human Rights Council ([88], p. 3), noted *with concern* within its resolution that "incidence and risk of child, early and forced marriage is highly exacerbated in humanitarian settings". This phenomenon was similarly acknowledged by the Committee to the Rights of the Children (2007, p. 4) who emphasised that conflict situations "combined with extreme poverty, drought and famine" are key factors contributing to

> …the significant number of street children and internally displaced children who are particularly vulnerable to all forms of exploitation, including acts covered by the Optional Protocol…that children may resort to prostitution and/or are forced into early marriages as a means for survival in exchange of food, money, or basic goods.

Children who in situations of forced displacement have become separated from their families, are considered, however, among the world's most vulnerable [89]. More so, unaccompanied minors,[1] whether internally displaced or seeking asylum outside of their country of origin, are often under-reported in official documents. The precise nature of the scale of the problem is, thus, elusive. This point will be discussed further in the succeeding chapter.

In situations where families are forcibly displaced, stateless, or living in poverty, child marriage is often arranged to ease financial burdens for the child bride's family, as well as, to secure an economic future for the girl [90]. This fact might not be surprising given the economic aspects of child marriage. However, the exacerbation of child marriages in fragile states, as in the case of Syrian refugee girls in Jordan, also occurs in response to familial fears and anxieties of risks such as "rape and sexual violence, unwanted pre-marital pregnancies, family shame and dishonour, homelessness, and hunger or starvation" within vulnerable environments such as refugee camps ([45], p. 7). As a result of these pressures and perceptions, child

[1] The term "unaccompanied minors" is used both by UNICEF and the UNHCR to refer to persons who are under 18 years of age or under a country's legal age of majority, are separated from both parents, and are not with and being cared for by a guardian or other adult who by law or custom is responsible for them. This includes minors who are without any adult care, minors who are entirely on their own, minors who are with minor siblings but who, as a group, are unsupported by any adult responsible for them, and minors who are with informal foster families. UN General Assembly (1997). Retrieved from http://www.un.org/documents/ga/docs/52/plenary/a52-273.htm.

marriage is considered a "protective tool against such risks (whether real or received)" ([45], p. 17). Notably, in countries in the Middle East and North Africa where child marriage is usually accepted or practiced during peacetime, the prevalence of the practice increases during conflict [25]. This has particularly occurred among Syrian refugees since the onset of the civil war. Prior to the Syrian Civil war, it was estimated that 13% of Syrian girls under 18 years of age were married [41].

In Jordan, most child marriages involve Syrian refugee girls [24]. Child marriages among Syrian refugee children in Jordan occur within the gaps of formal political and religious customary laws and practice. In these systems and liminal spaces of geography and law, vulnerable Syrian refugee girls in Jordan experience limited opportunities to participate in legal, political, and social forums which consequently affect their mobility, autonomy, and human rights [2, 45]. Data pertaining to accurate child marriage rates in conflict-affected states like Syria are, however, very challenging to ascertain due to "lack of marriage registrations and difficulties in obtaining valid information about population size" ([44], p. 54). In many ways this masks the extent of the problem facing vulnerable children. Since 2014 to 2018, child marriage among Syrian refugees had more than doubled, rising from 15% in 2014 to 36% in 2018 [3]. Recent data indicates that approximately 1 in 5 girls living in Za'atari refugee camp in Jordan—the largest refugee camp in the Middle East—are married before the age of 18 [53]. As presented in Chapter One of this book, children being forced to marry within contexts of refugee camps is perhaps emblematic of Said's discussion of the displaced person's need for cultural preservation during exile, even if such actions have negative implications for children. Here, displaced communities that continue to prescribe to conservative gender roles and patriarchal attitudes, may, thus, be seen as a way of maintaining and securing "community relations, a family's social standing and cultural traditions" ([25], p. 31).

In some cases, child marriages in Jordan may be temporary or for 'pleasure' [24, 40]. Here, wealthy older men, particularly those from Gulf countries, take Syrian refugee girls and sexually exploit them under the religious-based guise of 'marriage' for short periods of time, with the intent to later invalidate the marriage [24, 40]. Additionally, the often-desperate need for short-term financial stability may sometimes lead to circumstances where child marriages in Jordan are performed in unofficial capacities by unauthorised individuals, such as lawyers, as opposed to being formally officiated by sheikhs within *Sharia* courts (Laub [35]; [58]). In these circumstances, unofficial marriages are not formally recognised by the Jordanian government nor able to be registered within the Jordanian system, thereby further exposing child brides to the risk of lack of legal protection.

Conclusively, the problem of child marriage, and its impact on girls, may be framed as one of the failings of international laws and norms to protect vulnerable children (see [98, 42, 50, 72]). As discussed within this chapter, fragile states and conflict zones particularly exacerbate "the vulnerability of children to sale and sexual exploitation in such scenarios" ([97], p. 13). Conceptually, within international law, 'fragile' states refer to states where "a government cannot or will not act on its responsibility to protect and fulfil the rights of the majority of the population, particularly the most vulnerable" ([45], 6). The effectiveness of instruments such as the Optional Protocol to the Convention on the Rights of the Child on the Sale of Children, Child Prostitution and Child Pornography (OPSC) are, thus, challenged during crisis situations, and its weaknesses become evident. According to the provisions contained within Article 9(1) of the OPSC 'particular attention' should be given to "protect children who are especially vulnerable" to practices, such as, child marriage, and sexual exploitation and abuse [86]. The OPSC widens its definition of those who are especially vulnerable to also include children living in 'street situations', migrant and minority children, and children living in remote areas ([12], p. 12). In 2016, the fourth Special Rapporteur Dr. Najat Maala M'jid, also discussed the importance of creating safe spaces for displaced children in neighbouring countries within temporary shelters or camps [97]. At the same time, M'jid (cited in [97], p. 13) unveiled substantial international protection gaps that exist due to "the absence of a comprehensive framework for the coordination and allocations of roles and responsibilities of multiple international and local responders" to conflicts. M'jid (cited in [97], p. 13) specifically considered the lack of coherent processes in registering children before and after a disaster event as a factor that increases their risk of "being sold, exploited or illegally removed from their families and communities", as well, as increases the chances of children being forced into an illegal marriage.

Within a refugee context, such protective laws and frameworks are essential for children in the advent that they are separated from their families when fleeing conflict or disaster. In the case of child marriage, parents may not necessarily have their child's best interests at heart, and thus a child who is already vulnerable is made more so by being forced into marriage by their parent. Significantly, this issue remains prevalent. In addition, terms such as 'early' and even 'forced' marriage are not helpful when used within children's rights discourses or prevention strategies against child abuse. Indeed, Nour [47] argues that the vagueness of these terms used without context obscures the harrowing nature and extent of the issue and detracts from who the victims are. The importance of consistent use of clear and unambiguous terminology within international law when discussing child sexual abuse and child marriage is also recognised by Greijer and Doek [17] who argue that language (including what words are used or not used) impacts on how the issue is understood, what policy responses are considered, how data is collected, and even how legislation may emerge and be framed. When considering the issue of child marriage among refugee populations living in cross-border communities, the issue of language takes on more magnitude. What is considered 'young' in one culture, for example, may have a different meaning in another. Language and culture are, thus, significant aspect within human rights discourses and strategy responses [47].

References

1. Ahmed S, Khan S, Alia M, Noushad S (2013) Psychological impact evaluation of early marriages. Int J Endorsing Health Sci 1(2):84–86

2. Ahmed T, Sen B (2018) Conservative outlook, gender norms and female wellbeing: evidence from rural Bangladesh. World Dev 111(1):41–58
3. Al Jazeera (2018) Child marriage on the rise among Syrian refugee girls in Jordan. Al Jazeera. https://www.aljazeera.com/videos/2018/4/18/child-marriage-on-the-rise-among-syrian-refugee-girls-in-jordan
4. Alsaud FF (2015) Children's rights: Syrian refugee camps…childhood underfire? J Polit Law 8(3):228–237. https://doi.org/10.5539/jpl.v8n3p228
5. An-Na'im AA (ed) (1992) Human rights in cross-cultural perspectives: a quest for consensus. University of Pennsylvania Press, Philadelphia, USA
6. Andresen S, Ben-Arieh A (2016) Can we compare children's well-being across countries? Lessons from the children's worlds study. In: Hunner-Kreisel C, Bohne S (eds) Childhood, youth and migration: connecting global and local perspectives. Springer, Switzerland, pp 15–30
7. Archard, D. (2001). Philosophical Perspectives on Childhood. In J. Fionda (ed.), *Legal Concepts of Childhood*, 43–56. Oxford, UK: Hart Publishing
8. Baghdassarian A (2017) Negotiating human rights abuses through the moral foundations theory: an attempt to understand the moral motivations behind the male guardianship system in Saudi Arabia, female genital modification, and child marriage (CMC Senior Chapter, Claremonth McKenna College). Retrieved from: https://scholarship.claremont.edu/cmc_theses/1473/
9. Belhaj F, Soliman A, Kalle M (2021) MENA must take bold action against gender-based violence (GBV). World Bank. https://blogs.worldbank.org/arabvoices/mena-must-take-bold-action-against-gender-based-violence-gbv
10. Ben-Arieh A, Shimon E (2014) Subjective well-being and perceptions of safety among Jewish and Arab children in Israel. Child Youth Serv Rev 44:100–107
11. Bloxham L (2021) The feminisation of poverty: why gender matters. Concern. https://www.concern.org.uk/news/feminisation-poverty-why-gender-matters
12. Cedrangolo U (2009) The optional protocol to the convention on the rights of the child on the sale of children, child prostitution and child pornography and the jurisprudence of the committee on the rights of the child. (Innocenti Working Paper No. 2009–03). UNICEF Innocenti Research Centre, Florence, Italy
13. Cislaghi B, Denny EK, Cissé M, Gueye P, Shrestha B, Shrestha PN, Ferguson G, Hughes C, Clark CJ (2019) Changing social norms: the importance of "organized diffusion" for scaling up community health promotion and women empowerment interventions. Prev Sci 20(6):936–946. https://doi.org/10.1007/s11121-019-00998-3
14. Efevbera Y, Bhabha J (2020) Defining and deconstructing girl child marriage and applications to global public health. BMC Public Health 20(1547). https://doi.org/10.1186/s12889-020-09545-0
15. Fattore, T., Mason, J. & Watson, E. (2009). When Children are Asked About Their Well-being: Towards a Framework for Guiding Policy. Child Ind Res 2, 57–77. https://doi.org/10.1007/s12187-008-9025-3
16. Girls Not Brides (2017) The case for a minimum age for marriage [Brief]. https://www.girlsnotbrides.org/documents/709/Why-a-minimum-age-of-marriage-of-18.pdf
17. Greijer S, Doek J (2016) Terminology guidelines for the protection of children from sexual exploitation and sexual abuse. ECPAT International, Thailand
18. Haj-Yahia MM (2003) Beliefs about wife beating among Arab men from Israel: The influence of their patriarchal ideology. J Family Violence 18(4):193–206. https://doi.org/10.1023/A:1024012229984
19. Harrison A (2023) Evidence review: child marriage interventions and research from 2020 to 2022. Child Marriage Research to Action Network (CRANK). https://www.girlsnotbrides.org/documents/1904/CRANK_Evidence_review_Child_marriage_interventions__research_2020-22.pdf
20. Hart J (2016) Fear of female sexuality: addressing an unspoken driver of early and child marriage. Retrieved from: https://www.girlsnotbrides.org/articles/fear-of-female-sexuality-unspoken-driver-child-marriage/

21. Herring J (2012) Vulnerability, children, and the law. In: Freedman M (ed) Law and childhood studies, vol 14. Oxford University Press, UK, pp 243–263
22. Human Rights Watch (2013) Q & A: child marriage and violations of girls' rights. Retrieved from: https://www.hrw.org/news/2013/06/14/q-child-marriage-and-violations-girls-rights#3
23. Hunersen K, Attal B, Jeffery A, Metzler J, Alkibsi T, Elnakib S, Robinson WC (2021) Child marriage in Yemen: a mixed methods study in ongoing conflict and displacement. J Refug Stud 3(4):4551–4571. https://doi.org/10.1093/jrs/feaa144
24. International Catholic Migration Commission (ICMC) (2021) Child marriage in Jordan: report on project findings and recommendations. ICMC & Raskob Foundation for Catholic Activities Inc., Amman
25. International Centre for Research on Women (ICRW) & United Nations Children's Fund (UNICEF) (2017) Child marriage in the Middle East and North Africa. ICRW & UNICEF, Amman, Jordan
26. International Labour Organisation (ILO) (1973) Minimum age convention (No. 138)
27. International NGO Council on Violence Against Children (2016) 10 Years on: global progress & delay in ending violence against children—the rhetoric & the reality (Report 2016)
28. Irwin CE Jr (2011) A clear message: child marriage is a significant global problem requiring a collaborative, contextual, and evidence-based response. J Adolesc Health 69(6):871–872. https://doi.org/10.1016/j.jadohealth.2021.09.003
29. Kamal SMM, Hassan CH, Alam GM, Ying Y (2015) Child marriage in Bangladesh: trends and determinants. J Biosoc Sci 47(1):120–139. https://doi.org/10.1017/S0021932013000746
30. Kehris B (2022) Children affected by armed conflict and violence [Speech]. Office of the High Commissioner for Human Rights. https://www.ohchr.org/en/speeches/2022/07/children-affected-armed-conflict-and-violence
31. Kellie DJ, Blake KR, Brooks RC (2019) What drives female objectification? An investigation of appearance-based interpersonal perceptions and the objectification of women. PloS One 14(8). https://doi.org/10.1371/journal.pone.0221388
32. Kittay EF (2011) The ethics of care, dependence, and disability. Ratio Juris 24(1). https://doi.org/10.1111/j.1467-9337.2010.00473.x
33. Know Violence in Childhood (2017) Ending violence in childhood: overview [Global report 2017]. New Delhi, India
34. Landsdown G (2005) The evolving capacities of the child. UNICEF Innocenti Research Centre, Florence, Italy
35. Laub K (2017) Spike in number of Syrian teens marrying as child brides in Jordan. The Independent. https://www.independent.co.uk/news/world/middle-east/child-brides-jordan-syrian-teenage-refugees-a7880831.html
36. Lee Y (2013) Address: creating new futures for all children: the promise of international human rights law. Austr Int Law J 20(1):3–16
37. Lemmon GT, ElHarake LS (2014) Child brides, global consequences: how to end child marriage. Council on Foreign Relations, New York
38. Lotz M (2014) Parental values and children's vulnerability. In: Mackenzie C, Rogers W, Dodds S (eds) Vulnerability: new essays in ethics and feminist philosophy. Oxford University Press, New York, USA, pp 242–265
39. Mackenzie C, Rodgers W, Dodds S (2014) Introduction: what is vulnerability and why does it matter for moral theory? In Mackenzie C, Rodgers W, Dodds S (eds) Vulnerability: new essays in ethics and feminist philosophy. Oxford University Press, Oxford
40. Mason C, Smith C (2021) Married by exception: child marriage policies in the Middle East and North Africa. Save the Children International. https://resourcecentre.savethechildren.net/pdf/married_by_exception.pdf/
41. McGibney N, Haddad N (2020) Stolen future: war and child marriage in Northwest Syria. World Vision. https://www.wvi.org/sites/default/files/2020-07/Stolen%20Future-War%20and%20Child%20Marriage%20in%20Northwest%20Syria-Online.pdf
42. Mikhail S (2002) Child marriage and child prostitution: two forms of sexual exploitation. Gend Dev 10(1):43–49

43. Ministry of Justice of the Hashemite of Jordan (MoJJ) (1960) Penal code of Jordan, No. 16 (Unofficial English Translation). http://www.ahtnc.org.jo/sites/default/files/penal_code.pdf
44. Mourtada R, Schlecht J, DeJong J (2017) A qualitative study exploring child marriage practices among Syrian conflict-affected populations in Lebanon. Confl Heal 11(1):53–65. https://doi.org/10.1186/s13031-017-0131-z
45. Myers J (2013) Untying the knot: exploring early marriage in fragile states [Research Report]. World Vision UK, Milton Keynes, UK
46. Nassif G (2016) Syrian girls are being forced into child marriage in Lebanese refugee camps. The Wire. Retrieved from: https://thewire.in/women/syrian-girls-pushed-child-marriage-lebanese-refugee-camps.
47. Nour NM (2009) Child marriage: a silent health and human rights issue. Rev Obstet Gynecol 2(1):51–56
48. Oberg CN (2012) Embracing international children's rights: from principles to practice. Clin Pediatr 51(7):619–624. https://doi.org/10.1177/0009922811417302
49. Pais MS (2010) The protection of children from sexual exploitation optional protocol to the convention on the rights of the child on the sale of children, child prostitution and child pornography. Int J Child Rights 18(1):551–566. https://doi.org/10.1163/157181810X536815
50. Parker S (2015) Hidden crisis: violence against Syrian female refugees. Lancet 385(9985):2342–2342
51. Psaki SR, Melnikas AJ, Haque E, Saul G, Misunas C, Patel SK, Ngo T, Amin S (2021) What Are the drivers of child marriage? A conceptual framework to guide policies and programs. J Adolesc Health 69(6S):S13–S22. https://doi.org/10.1016/j.jadohealth.2021.09.001
52. Qamar AH (2022) Social value of the child. Contexts 21(1):40–45. https://doi.org/10.1177/15365042221083009
53. Quiroz S (2023) Syrian refugee women break the chain of child marriage. UNHCR Jordan. https://www.unhcr.org/jo/24029-syrian-refugee-women-break-the-chain-of-child-marriage.html
54. Rafferty Y (2013) International dimensions of discrimination and violence against girls: a human rights perspective. J Int Women's Stud 14(1):1–23
55. Revaz CR (2001) The optional protocols to the UN convention on the rights of the child on sex trafficking and child soldiers. Human Rights Brief 9(1):13–16
56. Roy A (2004) Peace and the new corporate liberation theology [2004 Sydney Peace Prize Lecture, University of Sydney]. Retrieved from: https://sydney.edu.au/news/84.html?newsstoryid=279
57. Russell AM (2014) "Victims of trafficking": the feminisation of poverty and migration in the gendered narratives of human trafficking. Societies 4(4):532–548. https://doi.org/10.3390/soc4040532
58. Save the Children (2014) Too young to wed: the growing problem of child marriage among Syrian girls in Jordan. Save the Children, London, UK
59. Save the Children (2016) Every last girl: free to live, free to learn, free from harm. Save the Children, London, UK
60. Save the Children (2021) Child marriage kills more than 60 girls a day [Press release]. Retrieved from: https://www.savethechildren.net/news/child-marriage-kills-more-60-girls-day
61. Save the Children, United Nations Children's Fund (UNICEF), & United Nations Global Compact (UNGC) (2012) Children's rights and business principles. https://resourcecentre.savethechildren.net/pdf/5717.pdf/
62. Scarpa S (2006) Child trafficking: international instruments to protect the most valuable victims. Fam Court Rev 44(3):429–447
63. Schroeder D, Gefenas E (2009) Vulnerability: too vague and too broad? Camb Q Healthc Ethics 18(2):113–121. https://doi.org/10.1017/S0963180109090203
64. Spencer D (2015) "To protect her honour"—child marriage in emergencies—the fatal confusion between protecting girls and sexual violence. In: Gender and protection in humanitarian contexts: critical issues series 1. Care International, UK

65. Swift J, Gould H (2021) Not an object: on sexualisation and exploitation of women and girls. UNICEF USA. https://www.unicefusa.org/stories/not-object-sexualization-and-exploitation-women-and-girls-0
66. The Sydney Morning Herald (2010) Yemen child forced into marriage dies. The Sydney Morning Herald. Retrieved from: https://www.smh.com.au/world/yemen-child-forced-into-marriage-dies-20100408-rvaj.html
67. Tobin J (2015) Understanding children's rights: vision beyond vulnerability. Nordic J Int Law 84(2):155–182
68. United Nations Children's Fund (UNICEF) (2005) Early marriage: a harmful traditional practice: a statistical exploration. UNICEF, New York, USA
69. United Nations Children's Fund (UNICEF) (2006) The state of the world's children 2007: women and children—the double dividend of gend*er Equality*. UNICEF, New York, USA
70. United Nations Children's Fund (UNICEF) (2012) Progress for children: a report card on adolescents (Report Number 10, April 2012). UNICEF, New York, USA
71. United Nations Children's Fund (UNICEF) (2014) A statistical snapshot of violence against adolescent girls. Author, New York, USA
72. United Nations Children's Fund (UNICEF) (2018) Current status + progress: child marriage is a violation of human rights, but is all too common. Retrieved from: https://data.unicef.org/topic/child-protection/child-marriage/
73. United Nations Population Fund (UNFPA) & United Nations Children's Fund (UNICEF) (2020) Child marriage and the law: technical note for the global programme to end child marriage. https://www.unicef.org/media/86311/file/Child-marriage-the-law-2020.pdf
74. United Nations Children's Fund (UNICEF) (2021a) Child protection advocacy briefing: violence against children. https://www.unicef.org/media/96686/file/VAC-Advocacy-Brief-2021.pdf
75. United Nations Children's Fund (UNICEF) (2021b) Towards ending child marriage: global trends and profiles of progress. UNICEF, New York
76. United Nations Children's Fund (UNICEF) (2022) Building back equal, with and for adolescent girls: a programme strategy for UNICEF 2022–2025. UNICEF, New York
77. United Nations Children's Fund (UNICEF) (2023) Child marriage (V1.15) .Retrieved from: https://data.unicef.org/topic/child-protection/child-marriage/
78. United Nations Children's Fund (UNICEF) (2023a) Is an end to child marriage within reach? Latest trends and future prospects. UNICEF, New York
79. United Nations Committee on the Rights of the Child (CRC) (2007) Consideration of reports submitted by states parties under Article 12(1) of the optional protocol to the convention on the rights of the child on the sale of children, child prostitution and child pornography: concluding observations, Sudan (Forty-fifth session, CRC/C/OPSC/SDN/CO/1)
80. United Nations Committee on the Rights of the Child (2013) General comment No. 14 (2013) on the right of the child to have his or her best interests taken as a primary consideration (art. 3, para. 1) [UN Doc. CRC /C/GC/14, Sixty-second session]
81. United Nations Department of Public Information (UNDPI) (2000) The Feminisation of poverty (DPI/2035/A). Retrieved from: http://www.un.org/womenwatch/daw/followup/session/presskit/fs1.htm
82. United Nations Economic and Social Commission for Western Asia (ESCWA) (2015) Child marriage in humanitarian settings in the Arab region: dynamics, challenges and policy options. ESCWA, New York, USA
83. United Nations General Assembly (1962) Convention on consent to marriage, minimum age for marriage and registration of marriages [Resolution 1763 A (XVII)]. Retrieved from: https://www.ohchr.org/sites/default/files/convention.pdf
84. United Nations General Assembly (1948) Universal declaration of human rights. http://www.ohchr.org/EN/UDHR/Documents/UDHR_Translations/eng.pdf
85. United Nations General Assembly (1989) Convention on the rights of the child (Treaty Series, 1577, 3). http://www.ohchr.org/Documents/ProfessionalInterest/crc.pdf

86. United Nations General Assembly (2000) Optional protocol to the convention on the rights of the child on the sale of children, child prostitution and child pornography. Retrieved from: http://www.ohchr.org/Documents/ProfessionalInterest/crc-sale.pdf.
87. United Nations General Assembly (2015) Resolution adopted by the general assembly on 25 September 2015: transforming our world: the 2030 agenda for sustainable development [UN Doc. A/RES/70/1, Seventeenth session]
88. United Nations General Assembly (2017) Resolution adopted by the Human Rights Council on 22 June 2017 (35/16): child, early and forced marriage in humanitarian settings. [UN Doc. A/HRC/RES/35/16, Thirty-fifth session]
89. United Nations High Commissioner for Refugees (UNHCR) (2017) Global trends: forced displacement in 2016. UNHCR, Geneva, Switzerland
90. United Nations High Commissioner for Refugees (UNHCR) (2017a) UNHCR age, gender and diversity: accountability report 2016. Author, Geneva, Switzerland
91. United Nations Population Fund (UNFPA) (2012) Marrying too young: end child marriage. UNICEF, New York, USA
92. United Nations Office of Drugs and Crime (UNODC) (2021) Killings of women and girls by their intimate partner or other family members: global estimates 2020 (Data Matter Series, No. 3). https://www.unodc.org/documents/data-and-analysis/statistics/crime/UN_BriefFem_251121.pdf
93. World Health Organisation (WHO) (2022) Violence against children. Retrieved from: https://www.who.int/news-room/fact-sheets/detail/violence-against-children
94. World Health Organisation (WHO) (2023) Adolescent and young adult health. Retrieved from: https://www.who.int/news-room/fact-sheets/detail/adolescents-health-risks-and-solutions
95. World Vision (2022) Child marriage: facts, FAQs, and how to help end it. https://www.worldvision.org/child-protection-news-stories/child-marriage-facts.
96. Wyn J, White R (1997) Rethinking youth. Allen & Unwin, NSW, Australia
97. de Boer-Buquicchio M (2016) 25 Years of fighting the sale and sexual exploitation of children: addressing new challenges. OHCHR, Geneva, Switzerland
98. de Silva-de-Alwis R (2007) Child marriage and the law: legislative reform initiative [Working Paper Series]. United Nations Children's Fund (UNICEF), New York, USA

Chapter 3
International Rights and Protections of the Refugee Child

Refugees have long been the focus of international law. Despite this, existing legal and governmental frameworks related to the protection of child refugees appear to be failing. This may be ascertained by the prevalent high rates of forced child marriages, as seen among Syrian refugees in Jordan. This chapter focuses on the legal frameworks that exist for the protection of refugees, and how they might, or not, protect refugee children from being forced into marriage.

The universal right for humans to seek and enjoy asylum from persecution in other countries is one of the key provisions of the 1948 Universal Declaration of Human Rights (UDHR), as noted within Article 14 [47]. The UDHR is a milestone instrument that was drafted and adopted following the inception of the UN. It presently remains one of the most important texts within international human rights law. It was, however, the UN 1951 Convention Relating to the Status of Refugees (hereafter, the '1951 Refugee Convention'), that became the "centrepiece of international refugee protection" ([50], p. 2). Grounded in Article 14 of the UDHR, the 1951 Refugee Convention sought, first and foremostly, to delineate special protections for unique groups of displaced persons seeking asylum by providing a comprehensive, internationally recognised, definition of a 'refugee'. Per Article 1(a)(2) of the 1951 Refugee Convention, a refugee is defined as any person who

> …owing to well-founded fear of being persecuted for reasons of race, religion, nationality, membership of a particular social group or political opinion, is outside the country of his nationality and is unable or, owing to such fear, is unwilling to avail himself of the protection of that country; or who, not having a nationality and being outside the country of his former habitual residence … is unable or, owing to such fear, is unwilling to return to it. ([48], p. 14).

The 1951 Refugee Convention also outlines the rights, and legal protection and assistance refugees are entitled to receive, and the obligations of states towards them ([39], p. 22). The UNHCR is deemed the 'guardian' of the 1951 Refugee Convention which was established in 1950, following the aftermath of WWII [56]. As a post-WWII instrument, however, the 1951 Refugee Convention was "originally limited in scope to persons fleeing events occurring before 1 January 1951 and within

S. Strungaru, *The Hidden Child Brides of the Syrian Civil War*,
SpringerBriefs in Law, https://doi.org/10.1007/978-981-97-2159-7_3

Europe" ([50], p. 2). The 1951 Refugee Convention has since been subject to only one amendment in the form of the 1967 Protocol which "removed the geographic and temporal limits" of the original text, thereby giving the Convention "universal coverage" ([50], p. 2).

According to international refugee law, an asylum seeker is a person who has sought or applied for either legal or physical international protection as a refugee and fled their country of origin for fear of persecution. This means that an asylum seeker's "claim for refugee status has not yet been determined" or assessed as qualifying to the provisions of refugee status, as stipulated within the 1951 Refugee Convention ([40], p. 2). States are nonetheless responsible for the protection of asylum seekers in their territory, as part of their "internationally recognised obligations to protect refugees on their territories" ([52], p. 5). Should a state find an asylum seeker to not be a "refugee or to not be in need of international protection" they may be sent back to their country of origin ([39], p. 1). Where "mass displacement usually makes individual refugee status determination impracticable" the UNHCR ([49], p. 1) presents a *prima facie* response framework in which 'temporary protection' can be granted to groups seeking asylum based on "obvious refugee characteristics of the individuals concerned". In this way, individual procedures under the 1951 Refugee Convention can be kept 'on hold' for use if or when it becomes "necessary to determine individual protection needs and consequent state responsibilities" ([49], p. 1).

Unlike refugees, and to an extent, asylum seekers, who are universally recognised under international law, there is no "universally accepted definition" nor legal concept of what constitutes a 'displaced person' or 'forced migrant' ([53], online). 'Forced migrants' are those who have been displaced or have experienced "involuntary movement … both across international borders and inside a single country" for reasons including "environmental disasters, conflict, famine, poverty or lack of opportunities and resources, or large-scale development projects" [53]. Relevant to discussion within Chapter One of this book, the UNHCR [53] iterates the importance of keeping a clear distinction between 'refugees' and 'migrants' so as to "maintain clarity in regard to the causes and nature of refugee movements and a state's specific obligations owed to refugees under international law". Furthermore, an 'internally displaced person' (IDP) refers to an individual who has fled their home or community for reasons similar to those of refugees, however, they continue to reside within the borders of their home countries. This definition suggests that IDPs may continue to be under the protection of their national government even in situations where their internal displacement is in fact a result of the actions of their government [39]. Unfortunately, because IDPs remain in inside the borders of their country of origin, they do not qualify for the same legal protections that are afforded to refugees; as Peer and the Refugee Council of Australia ([39], p. 1) clarify, "a person cannot be formally recognised as a refugee unless they are outside their home country". For this reason, IDPs often experience heightened exposure to physical vulnerability and insecurity, and emotional responses such as helplessness and stress.

Presently, there is no one universal instrument for the specific protection of refugee children from forced marriage. Rather, the protections of vulnerable children from devasting gender-based practices, such as child marriage, are referred to within several key international texts, together with the protections stipulated in the above-noted instruments. The most prominent international human rights instruments detailing states' responsibilities for protecting children against forced marriage includes the 1948 UDHR, the United Nations Convention on the Elimination of All Forms of Discrimination against Women [38], the UN Convention on the Rights of the Child [60] (CRC), the UN Optional Protocol to the Convention on the Rights of the Child on the Sale of Children, Child Prostitution and Child Pornography [61] (OPSC), as well as the Convention on Consent to Marriage, Minimum Age for Marriage and Registration of Marriages [59]. Of the above-listed instruments, the UDHR is perhaps the most contentious as it does not contain an explicit prohibition against child marriage per se. Reference to 'marriage' is made within Article 16 of the UDHR stipulating that "Men and women of full age, without any limitation due to race, nationality or religion, have the right to marry and to found a family. They are entitled to equal rights as to marriage, during marriage and at its dissolution" ([47], p. 74). Gaffney-Rhys ([13], p. 363) argues, however, that the wording contained within this clause, referring to 'men and women' rather than 'males and females' and neither 'boys' or 'girls', was intended to provide guidance for the prevention of child marriages, and address the practice as appropriate to a target age group.

The ratification of these instruments by member-states constitutes a commitment to introduce or amend its own internal policies and laws to reflect the provisions of the corresponding international instrument [13]. The protections stipulated within these instruments address, first and foremost, the right of the relevant parties to exercise "free and full" consent in the marriage decision ([47], p. 74). This clause suggests that such consent can only be made in the capacity in which the parties involved in marriage are "sufficiently mature to make an informed decision about a life partner" ([45], p. 1). Article 16 of the Convention on the Elimination of All Forms of Discrimination Against Women (CEDAW), provides additional clarification stating that "the betrothal and the marriage of a child shall have no legal effect, and all necessary action, including legislation, shall be taken to specify a minimum age for marriage" ([38], p. 7). Clarification for the minimum age for marriage was subsequently presented by the Committee for on the Elimination of Discrimination Against Women in 1994 within Article 36 of its General Recommendation No. 21 in which "the minimum age for marriage should be 18 years for both man and woman" ([46], p. 8). This is in line with the CRC [60] that defines a child as an individual under the age of 18 years.

While most states have ratified both the CEDAW Convention [38] and CRC [38], their implementation within national jurisdictions nonetheless remain slow and unclear [18]. In the Middle East and North African region, for example, these protection instruments are currently at various stages of legislative implementation and significant changes in social norms relating to child marriages and gender-based violence are yet to be wholly enforced. In Jordan, under the Jordanian 'Personal Status Law', the legal minimum age for marriage for both boys and girls is 18 years

[32]. In 2017, however, exceptions to the legal minimum age of marriage were introduced. According to the new regulations, children below the age of 16 can receive judicial consent to be married on the condition that "there is no more than a 15 year age difference between the bride and groom", "the groom has no other wives, and the bride can continue her education"; and until the judges are satisfied that the groom and bride are religiously and financially prepared for the marriage ([32], p. 12).

Arguably, barriers in the adoption of international treaties, particularly within the Middle East and North Africa occur, because of cultural differences between western and non-western jurisdictions [13]. In other words, international efforts to address and end the practice of child marriage are based on western assumptions of childhood and adolescence which often ignore the cultural complexity of the issue [13]. As Bridgeman and Monk ([6], cited in Gaffney-Rhys [13], p. 368) point out, the term 'child' is "not a universally defined concept". Furthermore, provisions contained within global instruments may too be seen to be ambiguous and may further complicate regional judicial responses. For example, despite the CEDAW expressly forbidding child marriage, it does not actually provide a definition of a child, likewise, while a definition of a child is contained with the CRC, it does not make express reference to the practice of child marriage [13]. As a result, various states may inevitably interpret and adhere to each instrument differently [13]. What necessarily emerges is an unclear international policy framework regarding which age- and gender-specific patterns of sexual, marital, and reproductive transitions should be viewed as problematic. As such, "obtaining worldwide agreement to a set of wide-ranging norms", continues to prove challenging, particularly when culture and religion that are embedded in patriarchal values and attitudes have prevailing social, legal, and political influence within states like Jordan ([13], p. 368). Gaffney-Rhys [13] suggests that instead of a universal doctrine as the basis for introducing age of marriage consent law, a regional approach may be more appropriate among states that share similar cultural, political, and economic, systems. One such example, is the 1990 African Charter on the Rights and Welfare of the Child developed by the African ([2], p. 18) which comprehensively declares within Article 21 both the explicit prohibition of "child marriage and betrothal of girls and boys", and that "effective action, including legislation, be taken to specify the minimum age of marriage to be eighteen years".

At its core, international law seeks to establish and set internationally accepted normative standards about 'peace', 'justice', and 'human rights' [30]. For Koskenniemi ([30], p. 29), international law exists as "encouragement for political transformation". With regard to child marriage, the UN presently continues to draw attention to the practice as both a human rights violation, and a direct manifestation of gender-based inequality, through the lens of its 1966 international covenants on civil and political rights, as well as, economic, social and cultural rights. While international law cannot guarantee a reduction in child marriage incidences, it can nonetheless promote accountability for those nations who have ratified conventions, resolutions, and protocols, ultimately committed to the eradication of the practice [13]. As Rafferty argued a decade ago, an international human rights framework is "crucial in the struggle against harmful cultural or traditional practices and gender-based cultural and social norms" (Rafferty [41], p. 3). For girls in particular, practices such as child marriage "preserves the lower status accorded to [them] and brutally affects their experiences of childhood" (Rafferty [41], p. 3).

3.1 Refugee Status Laws in Jordan: Safe Haven or Vulnerable Spaces?

The displacement crisis in Syria that has occurred since 2011 as a result of the prolonged civil war, has led to the mass exodus of Syrians to neighbouring countries including Jordan, Lebanon, and Turkey. According to Kaya [28], the nature of, and perceptions regarding, the Syrian asylum among its neighbouring states are commonly shaped by a shared amicable 'welcome culture' [28]. Based on the Islamic notion of *Ansar* meaning 'hospitality' or 'benevolence', over the last decade, states like Jordan have perceived forcibly displaced Syrian as 'guests', welcoming them into their countries [28]. For Kaya [28], this hospitality is rooted in traditional values of 'Muslim fraternity' and Arabic culture. While Jordan has been "praised for its open-border policy and humanitarian stance towards Syrian refugees" ([1], p. 3), Jordan is neither a signatory to the UN 1951 Refugee Convention on Refugees nor its subsequent 1967 Protocol, as such, refugee-specific directives in Jordanian law lack a coherent framework. From a sociolegal perspective, this means that Jordan lacks clear national legislation and a legal framework for dealing with refugees or mechanisms for dealing with refugees' legal status determination while entering Jordanian borders [3, 10, 29]. By responding to the Syrian refugee crisis with a discourse of 'Ansar', Jordanian efforts to accommodate and assist its displaced Syrian neighbours are, thus, observably based on a 'religious and charity-based' duty rather than a 'humanitarian responsibility' as a UN member-state [28]. For Kaya [28], the observed hospitality of the Jordanian government and its citizens toward Syrian asylum seekers suggests a conditional response on the basis of 'temporality'. For the International Labour Organisation (ILO), Jordan's non-signatory status raises multiple concerns, including

> … the politically and socially complex – and yet unresolved – Palestinian refugee issue; popular sentiment against refugee integration; lack of resources and capacity to provide for refugees; and misinformation about the perceived social and economic burden of refugees and related questions of national security. ([20], p. 11)

At the same time, gaps within international refugee law may also be arguably observed. As introduced in this chapter, according to Article 14 of the UDHR [47], "everyone has the right to seek and to enjoy in other countries asylum from persecution". While this provision is globally recognised and foundational to human rights, no international instrument contains a definition of 'asylum', nor is it mentioned within the 1951 Refugee Convention [5]. Notably, the absence of the term 'asylum' within the 1951 Refugee Convention also inevitably precludes any provisions within the text with regard to the requirement for states to establish a refugee status procedure, nor does it stipulate minimum procedural standards [5]. As is the case with Jordan, this suggests that the granting of asylum to displaced populations is exercised at the discretion of individual states and this discretion may, consequently, inconsistently vary between countries [5]. Procedural guarantees available to those seeking refugee status also vary between countries, including legal aid, and the right to appeal revoked protection status, refused protection or a human rights claim [5]. In this way, the 1951 Refugee Convention only protects persons who meet the criteria for refugee status [54].

Notably, the Government of Jordan itself does not grant refugee status to asylum seekers per se. Rather the Government of Jordan works in collaboration with the UNHCR to help process and register displaced persons that have crossed the Jordanian border. This collaboration is the result of a signed agreement between the UNHCR and Jordan, formalised by the 1998 Memorandum of Understanding (MoU) [16], which established parameters for cooperation with regard to the issue of refugees and asylum seekers. One of the key outcomes of the MoU involves processes of refugee registration, and subsequent categorisation and prioritisation, that are undertaken by the UNHCR. The process of registering refugees is considered one of the most imperative activities by the UNHCR in the fulfillment of its core mandate of protection [55]. Registration is a necessity in providing refugees access to assistance and ensuring their freedom of movement. It also allows the UNHCR to help identify vulnerabilities or specifically vulnerable cohorts who can be referred to UNHCR partners for additional support [55]. Following their arrival into Jordan, Syrian refugees are issued with a 'Proof of Registration' card by the UNHCR which confirms their status and residency in camps [11, 36]. The UNHCR is also responsible with the issuance of 'asylum seeker certificates' which allows Syrian refugees access to national public services and systems such as primary schools for children and subsidized healthcare [11, 36]. Asylum seeker certificates are valid for one year, subject to annual renewal[1] [3].

In Jordan, the MoU has allowed for the implementation of continuous registration, and regular verification and update of data for all nationalities. Markedly, the 1998 MoU is the only refugee-specific directive in Jordan which importantly includes and recognises the 1951 Refugee Convention's definition of 'refugee', and accepts the principle of 'non-refoulement' in accordance with customary international law [20]. 'Non-refoulement' is a principle within international law that precludes states from forcibly returning refugees or asylum seekers to their country of origin where they deemed at risk of being subjected to persecution or torture. Reference to the principle of non-refoulement is also contained in the Jordanian Constitution ([14], art. 21(i)) which stipulates that "political refugees shall not be extradited on account of their political beliefs or for their defence of liberty". In line with the principle of non-refoulment, Jordanian Law No. 24 of the 1973 'Residency and Foreigners' Affairs

[1] This is based on the partial amendment of the MoU in 2014 which extended the refugee determination processing period from 30 to 90 days, and extended the validity of asylum seeker certifications from six months to one year [3].

Law' additionally grants the Jordanian Minister of Interior the right to exempt "the requirements for the entry and residence of foreign nationals" ([20], p. 11) to persons "on account of special considerations connected with international or humanitarian courtesy or of the right to political asylum or yet in application of the principle of reciprocity" ([15], art.29(h)).

Notably, one of the most critical provisions contained within No. 24 of the 1973 Jordanian 'Residency and Foreigners' Affairs Law' is that refugees are not automatically entitled to receive residency, work, education, or healthcare in the local communities [3]. According to law No. 24, non-Jordanians are required to obtain a 'residency permit' in order to be able to live and work in Jordan, subject to the Jordanian Ministry of Interior's (MoI) approval [3]. The MoI is a department of the Government of Jordan, primarily responsible for internal affairs and national law, order, and security. Since 2014, Jordanian authorities require all Syrians living outside of the camps in host-communities to register directly with the Jordanian MoI and be issued with a biometric service card (the 'MoI card') [11]. The MoI card is considered a particularly important legal document within Jordan's national law system as possession of an MoI card confirms that its holder is officially entitled to live outside of a refugee camp [36]. The MoI card is, however, only valid for use in areas where the card was initially registered. In this case, if refugees move from their initial place of registration, they must reapply for a new MoI from within their new location (IHRC & NRC, [19]). As such, the MoI card allows Syrians to register births, deaths, and marriage; allows the holder to apply for work permits and driver's licences; and allows the holder to access some local services [36]. Fabos ([12], p. 106), argues however, that Arab Middle Eastern states have adopted Western-style immigration policies that are "built on similar assumptions of state rights and refugees as out of place". According to Fabos ([12], p. 106), legal identity regimes, such as the Jordanian requirement for an MoI card, are, therefore, largely a function of what she conceptualises as "Westphalian border-making processes and the codification of national sovereignty" that are likely reactions to discursive threats posed by the refugee 'other'.

Recent international policy discussions are, however, no longer about Syrians' right to work in Jordan, but rather, "how and under what conditions" ([11], p. 9). Since 2016, following the initiation of the 'Jordan Compact', the Government of Jordan has provided an "innovative approach to dealing with protracted displacement" by facilitating improved access for Syrian refugees to legal employment in certain sectors ([11], p. 9). The 'Jordan Compact' is supported by concessional financing of millions of dollars in grants and loans as part of an economic and trade agreement initiative between Jordan and donor countries within the European Union [11]. According to the Durable Solutions Platform et al. ([11], p. 9), the compact represents "an opportunity for responsibility sharing between refugee hosting countries and the international community, and a step towards promoting medium- and longer-term solutions for Syrian refugees in Jordan". Certain initiatives supported by the Government of Jordan to improve Syrian refugee's access to the labour market have included "waiving the fees to obtain a work permit, simplifying the documentation requirements, and allowing the registration and operation of some home-based-businesses"

([11], p. 8). While considerable progress has been made, challenges remain. In 2022, only one-third of Syrian refugees hold a work permit, of which between 4 and 8% benefit from social insurance and security schemes [11]. Furthermore, refugees are typically employed in unskilled or low-skilled roles, that typically involve low wages, and expose Syrians to dangerous working conditions and vulnerability to exploitation [11].

To receive a new (or renewed) MoI Card, Syrian refugees must present the following key documents: proof of identity (such as a Syrian passport, identity card or birth certificate), UNHCR asylum-seeker certificates, a proof of address, and a health certificate obtained from an authorised health clinic in Jordan[36]. This occurs under a process called the 'Urban Verification Exercise' (UVE) which was introduced in 2015. There are, however, significant challenges faced by Syrian refugees in obtaining MoI Cards. In the first instance, to obtain an MoI Card every Syrian (including children) must be registered as a refugee with the UNHCR. Data provided by the Norwegian Refugee Council at the end of 2016 reveals that out of 515,000 UNHCR registered refugees living outside of camps, only 363,000 had obtained new MoI cards ([36], p. 4). For the majority of refugees, their reasons for being unable to access a MoI card is because of a lack of identity documents, and this particularly affects children [36]. In most cases, the lack of official Syrian documentation is due to documents being destroyed or lost in the Syria during the conflict [25]. Other reasons include the confiscation of documents by Jordanian authorities, or because Syrian refugees may have originated from parts of Syria where identity documents were unable to be produced [25]. Cases involving lack of documentation for children, in particular, are often because children were too young to have had identity documentation at the time of fleeing Syria to Jordan [25].

Nonetheless, without identity documentation such as birth certificates, for example, a child cannot be issued a Jordanian MoI card, and this has significant impacts The lack of civil documentation means that children are not only denied free movement and access to health and education, but they also face long-term restricted living within refugee camps, refoulement, or risk arrest and detention in juvenile centres. The precarious possibility of being forcibly returned back to Syria, despite their status as refugees in Jordan, particularly illustrates the resounding vulnerability Syrian children face in host countries, as well as overall risk of being killed when returning through territories that remain markedly unsafe in their home country. According to the Norwegian Refugee Council et al. ([37], p. 9), cases of "refoulement peaked in early 2017, with up to 400 [refugees] a month deported as the government cited security concerns". Contextually, despite the apparent lack of coherent framework regulating refugee admission into Jordan, the Jordanian Minister of Interior retains the overarching authority to issue regulations in relation to travel documentation that may be granted to non-Jordanian nationals, specifically, refugees [33]. In this regard, a policy of 'selective admission' is observed, and has been practiced predominantly on the rationale of maintaining national security. In June 2016, for example, Jordan officially closed its border with Syria and declared the area a 'closed military zone' following a suicide car bomb attack that killed six Jordanians [42, 43]. While national security has been a key element of Jordanian refugee practices, closing the border left 45,000 people, about 75% of whom were women and children, trapped in a remote demilitarised camp called the 'Berm', located in desert town of Rukban between the borders of Syria and Jordan [25]. This reaction is not surprising, for, as Chimni [9], highlights, the language of security within refugee discourse is arguably used to couch issues of burden-sharing, in other words, discourse that frames the perception that refugees place increased demand on scarce resources and threaten the security of regions within the host nation thereby justifies the erosion of fundamental principles such as that of non-refoulement.

For some Syrian refugee households, family members may often have mixed legal statuses thereby adding another layer of complexity. For example, some members might have full UNHCR and MoI registration, while others have either one or neither [25]. This creates challenging circumstances where different members are exposed to varying degrees of vulnerability and unequal access to services. This is often largely due to misinformation (or lack of information) regarding registration processes, despite Syrians demonstrating a clear understanding of the importance of legal and civil documentation with relation to their resettlement in Jordan [25]. In 2018, for example, the Agency for Technical Cooperation and Development (ACTED) found that 26% of Syrian refugee households in Jordan had at least one member who did not have an MoI card due to lack of information, despite being eligible [25]. Of further concern, without a MoI Card, births, marriages, and deaths are unable to be officially recorded [36]. In this way, Syrian women and girls who are unable to provide the necessary required documentation, may be at particular risk of gender-based risks and violence—such as child marriage.

While international law is clear in its stand for refugee rights and for the rights of the child, harmful human rights practices such as forced child marriage continues to occur, as seen in the case among Syrian child refugees who have sought asylum in the neighbouring state of Jordan. One of the most significant factors contributing to Syrian children's vulnerability is their lack of access to education, specifically because of the stringent identity requirements and processes in Jordan. While Syrian refugee children are entitled to the right to primary and secondary school education, disparities in school attendance persist [26]. This is particularly seen with regard to secondary school attendance among Syrian refugees. According to the Durable Solutions Platform et al. [11], only a quarter of Syrian refugee children of secondary school ages (16–18 years) are enrolled in Jordan while higher (tertiary) education is 'out of bounds'. For Krafft et al. [31], a refugee child's lack of access to education is likely closely linked to practices such as child marriage, beyond educational learning and literacy implications.

3.2 The Governmentality and Threat of the Refugee Camp

As of 2023, the UNHCR estimated that approximately 18.2% (135,031) of Syrian refugees live in designated refugee camps, with most living in Jordan's urban areas concentrated in Amman (the nation's capital), Irbid, and Al Mafraq [58]. The large majority of camped Syrian refugees live in either Za'atari (82,992) and Azraq (45,001) refugee camps. Opened in 2012, Za'atari camp is renowned for being the largest refugee camp in the world, and has since become a symbol of the long-running Syrian refugee crisis [8].

Although the concept of 'refugee camp' is invariably used within international law and public discourse, there is no internationally prescribed definition of the term itself [24]. This lack of clear definition of refugee camps, and lack of reference thereof within key legal documents such as the 1951 Refugee Convention, is, as Janmyr ([24], pp. 103–104) contends, "particularly disconcerting [as the] 'label' confers an array of legal, political, and bureaucratic implications for refugee protection". One of the most widely recognised and used operational definitions of 'camps' is found within the 'Camp Management Toolkit'—a publication endorsed by six international organisations, including the UNHCR. The 'Camp Management Toolkit' defines 'camps' as

> … temporary settlements including planned or self-settled camps, collective centres and transit and return centres established for hosting displaced persons. It applies to ongoing and new situations where due to conflict or natural disasters, displaced persons are compelled to find shelter in temporary places. ([35], p. 14)

The above definition, however, does not attempt to provide any clarification to the "underlying objectives of hosting individual in camps", particularly given that the broad term 'displaced person' is used to refer to both refugees and internally displaced persons (IDPs) ([24], p. 103). As previously mentioned within this book, while 'refugee' is a legally recognised status that grants individuals entitlement to international protection under international laws, IDPs on the other hand, are not afforded a legal status [24]. According to Janmyr [23], the approach outlined within the Camp Management Toolkit is, thus, 'descriptive' rather than 'normative'. In 2014, the UNHCR sought to expand upon, and provide further clarification, on the above-noted conceptualisation and definition of camps within its text, *Policy on Alternatives to Camps*, specifically with respect to refugees. The text notes that "camps are locations where refugees reside and where, in most cases, host governments and humanitarian actors provide assistance and services in a centralised manner" ([51], p. 4).

While the host state is generally seen as being primarily responsible for refugee camps, camps typically fall under the interdependent jurisdiction and administration of the host refugee state, the UNHCR, and UN partner agencies (often non-governmental organisations), with each authoritative body having various forms of responsibility [24]. Janmyr [24] describes the issue of responsibility of camp management, however, as a 'sliding scale', in the sense that camps are largely dependent on the host state's ability and willingness to provide effective protections. These protections include aspects of physical security of the camps themselves, the personal security of the refugees, as well as, protections that ensure the maintenance of the humanitarian implementation and character of the camps [22, 27]. A predominantly state-centric approach to camp management responsibility is attributed, in part, to the foundational principle of 'state sovereignty' within international law. In response to critiques suggesting that the involvement of international organisations, such as the UNHCR, "deprive the state of the capacity to govern a certain part of its territory", the principle of state sovereignty clarifies that camps are established only with the 'consent' of the host state and are, thus, not political signifiers of infringements upon state sovereignty ([24], p. 170). Although states have a legal obligation for the protection of individuals within their territory, refugee camps are, nonetheless, notorious for their insecurity.

The provision of safe shelter is a critical determinant for those in need of protection and is also important for human dignity [44]. Host states typically allocate areas of land to be used for designated camps which is most often privately owned and only sporadically state-owned land. The Sphere Project, initiated in 1997 by non-governmental humanitarian organisations, established a Humanitarian Charter outlining the minimum conditions required for refugee camps. The Charter considered that the provision of structurally safe housing with sufficient space, free from disease, that offer protection from the weather and provide sustainable access to clean water, heating, lighting, and sanitation are necessary requirements, as well, access to healthcare services, schools, and other social facilities, are all required for the safe livelihood of its occupants [44]. These provisions place the family institution as the principal unit for the organisation of refugee camps. In doing so, according to Bulley ([7], p. 75), the aim is to replicate systems that build and foster communities which, in turn, seek to reconceptualise camps from "spaces of government" into a community of "active and responsible individuals and families".

Bulley [7] assesses, however, that such initiatives are perhaps 'naïve' or 'misguided' forms of 'governmentality'. The concept of 'governmentality' in this context suggests that the conceputalisation of refugee camps through the lens of 'community' is arguably a "programme of government" that allows the state and its counterparts to exercise of a "very specific albeit complex form of power" ([34], p. 296). In this way, Bulley ([7], p. 75) argues that refugee camps are extraterritorial sites of biopolitics that employ "advanced liberalist methods of governing the global poor". Scholars including Bulley [7], Lipper [34], and Janmyr [24] purport more pragmatic perspectives of refugee camps as being liminal structures that merely maintain and manage "raw biological existence...without the politically qualified life possible within a community" ([7], p. 65, p. 69), existing as spaces between the 'temporary' and the 'permanent' ([23], p. 112). Apart from the infrastructure of refugee camps, the geospatial locations of camps further illustrate aspects of governmentality. As an 'informal' confinement mechanism, camps are typically located in poor, or remote or inhospitable areas, usually unused or uninhabited by the local population. They exist either in close vicinity to national borders or in places without transportation links, infrastructure, and basic services [24]. Located in the desert of northern Jordan, approximately 12 kms from the border with Syria, the Za'atari refugee camp in Jordan is an example that typifies these characteristics [4]. A study undertaken by Jabbara and Zara [20] investigated the impacts of the Syrian conflict on Syrian refugee children within the Za'atari camp vis-à-vis two control groups of children—one in the capital of Jordan, Amman, and another from the Jordanian Ramtha district in Jordan which is located across the border from Syria. The results of Jabbara and Zara's [20] study found that Syrian refugee children resident within Za'atari refugee camp were the only group to express symptoms of extreme depression and anxiety, including suicidal thoughts. Children residing in the Ramtha district also demonstrated considerable signs of distress, especially when compared with the group of children living in Amman [20]. As such, one of the key findings of the study illustrated that the further refugee children live away from the source of the conflict and hostilities that they sought asylum from, the more secure they appeared to feel and the fewer symptoms were evidenced, such as anxiety and depression [21].

The provisional design of refugee camps symbolically reflects the prevailing feature of the global refugee experience: spaces of insecurity and coexistence where previously unrelated people are placed together in need of urgent international assistance. The spatial and symbolic characteristics of the camps often produce, according to Bulley ([7], p. 73), "unexpected and unintentional outcomes, potential emergences of the new or novel". According to human rights organisations such as Save the Children and UNHCR, children are the most vulnerable within refugee camps because they are not only forced to leave behind their homes and key developmental institutions (such as family, friends, and schools), but are forced within unfamiliar environments surrounded by strangers. And yet, for a whole generation of children, the camp is not merely a liminal space but has become their whole world [57]. Ten years after the onset of the Syrian civil war, half the population of Jordan's Za'atari camp are children, many of whom have grown up without seeing outside of, or going beyond, the camp's borders [8]. Since opening in 2012, the UNHCR [57] has recorded over 20,000 births in Za'atari camp. Refugee camps are especially challenging for children particularly because of the common chronic difficulties associated with camp life. Such difficulties include minimal access to shelter, food, and water, overcrowding, unsecure and unhygienic facilities (including prefabricated shelters in need of maintenance), and continuous exposure to trauma (or those with trauma symptoms). As Jordan is the second most water-scare country in the world, water is a particularly precious resource within refugee camps, especially given their location in the arid desert-lands of northeast Jordan [8]. Although all shelters are connected to a water supply within Za'atari camp, UNHCR revealed that the water supply was only sufficient to cover the needs of 30% of the households [8].

While camps are seen as limiting to the rights and freedoms of its occupants, UNHCR initiatives, such as, the 2014 Policy on Alternatives to Camps and the 2009 Policy on Urban Refugees, seek to "promote the local integration of refugees within host nations as a 'rights-based approach' to refugee assistance, explicitly moving away from camps as the assumed foundation of refugee policy" ([17], p. 204). Local integration in this context furnishes refugees with the right to peacefully settle outside of camps and still be granted "full and permanent asylum, membership and residency status, by the host government … through a process of legal, economic, social and cultural incorporation, culminating in the offer of citizenship" ([23], p. 1). However, for many Syrian children in Jordan, data illustrates that this is sadly not the case. While there is a demonstrated commitment by the state of Jordan and the UN to harmoniously create safe spaces for Syrian refugees who have fled conflict, there nonetheless appears to be a discrepancy regarding the local measures in place for the protection of refugee children, particularly with regard to children's exposure to gender-based violence and harmful practices such as child marriage which remain concerningly prevalent in the present-day. The ongoing vulnerabilities faced by refugee children significantly demonstrates how refugee camps represent just one aspect of the multifaceted, complex contexts of displacement. As will be discussed in the following chapter, international strategies for the protection of refugees, generally, and the protection of women and children against human rights abuses, specifically, are not neutral processes. Rather, strategies for refugee protections are informed by historical, social, and cultural constructs that continue to influence human rights discourses and instruments, and influence international law outcomes.

References

1. Achilli L (2015) Syrian refugees in Jordan: a reality check. [Migration Policy Centre Policy Brief 2015/02]. European University Institute, Florence, Italy
2. African Union (1990) African charter on the rights and welfare of the child [Doc No. CAB/LEG/24.9/49]. 36804-treaty-african_charter_on_rights_welfare_of_the_child.pdf (au.int)
3. Al Qaralleh AS (2022) Jordan and Syrian humanitarian refugees' dilemma: international law perspective. Heliyon 8(5):1–11. https://doi.org/10.1016/j.heliyon.2022.e09377
4. Al Jazeera (2022) Mapping the largest Syrian refugee camp in the world. Al Jazeera. https://www.aljazeera.com/news/2022/7/28/mapping-the-largest-syrian-refugee-camp-in-the-world
5. Atak I, Crépeau F (2023) Asylum in the twenty-first century: trends and challenges. In: Triandafyllidou A (ed) Routledge handbook of immigration and refugee studies, 2nd edn. Routledge, New York, pp 396–404
6. Bridgeman, J., & Monk, D. (2000). Introduction: Reflections on the Relationship Between Feminism and Child Law. In J. Bridgeman and D. Monk (eds.), Feminist Perspectives on Child Law. London: Cavendish
7. Bulley D (2014) Inside the tent: community and government in refugee camps. Secur Dialouge 45(1):63–80. https://doi.org/10.1177/0967010613514788
8. Carlisle L (2022) Jordan's Za'atari refugee camp: 10 facts at 10 years. UNHCR. https://www.unhcr.org/news/stories/jordans-zaatari-refugee-camp-10-facts-10-years
9. Chimni B (2000) Globalisation, humanitarianism and the erosion of refugee protection. J Refug Stud 13(2):243–263
10. Clutterbuck M, Hussein Y, Mansour M, Rispo M (2021) Alternative protection in Jordan and Lebanon: the role of legal aid. Forced Migr Rev 67(1):52–56
11. Durable Solutions Platform (DSP), Development Initiatives, Save the Children, Danish Refugee Council (DRC), International Rescue Committee, Action Against Hunger (2022) Financing for protracted displacement: in the Syrian refugee context in Jordan. https://reliefweb.int/attachments/e9ee41b0-366c-3688-ae15-1e4f84391aeb/DI-DSP%20displacement%20financing%20-%20Jordan%202022.pdf
12. Fabos A (2015) Refugees in the Arab Middle East: academic and policy perspectives. Digest Middle East Stud 24(1):96–110
13. Gaffney-Rhys R (2011) International law as an instrument to combat child marriage. Int J Hum Rights 15(3):359–373. https://doi.org/10.1080/13642980903315398
14. Government of Jordan (GoJ) (1952) Constitution of the Hashemite kingdom of Jordan 1952, with amendment (2011) (Unofficial English Translation). Retrieved from: https://www.constituteproject.org/constitution/Jordan_2011
15. Government of Jordan (GoJ) (1973) Law no. 24 of 1973 on residence and foreigner's affairs. (Unofficial English Translation). Retrieved from: https://sherloc.unodc.org/cld/uploads/res/

document/law-no--24-of-1973-on-residence-and-foreigners-affairs_html/Law_No_23_of_1973_EN.pdf
16. Government of Jordan (GoJ) & UNHCR (1998) Memorandum of understanding. Retrieved from: http://carim-south.eu/databases/legal/Jordan/Bilateral%20Agreements/LE2JOR002_AREN.pdf
17. Hamill K (2017) Rights, refugees, and the case of Syria. In: Chase AT (ed) Routledge handbook on human rights and the Middle East and North Africa. Routledge, London, UK, pp 196–216
18. International Centre for Research on Women (ICRW) & United Nations Children's Fund (UNICEF) (2017) Child Marriage in the Middle East and North Africa. ICRW & UNICEF, Amman, Jordan
19. International Human Rights Clinic (IHRC) & Norwegian Refugee Council (NRC) (2015) Registering rights: Syrian refugees and the documentation of births, marriages, and deaths in Jordan. https://hrp.law.harvard.edu/wp-content/uploads/2015/11/Registering-rights-report-NRC-IHRC-October20151.pdf
20. International Labour Organisation (ILO) (2015) Access to work for Syrian refugees in Jordan: a discussion paper on labour and refugee laws and policies. ILO, Beirut, Lebanon
21. Jabbara SA, Zaza HI (2014) Impact of conflict in Syria on Syrian children at the Zaatari refugee camp in Jordan. Early Child Dev Care 184(9–10):1295–1530. https://doi-org.ezproxy.une.edu.au/10.1080/03004430.2014.916074
22. Jacobsen K (1999) A safety-first approach to physical protection in refugee camps (Working paper no. 4), Mellon Report Series, pp 1–18
23. Jacobsen K (2001) The forgotten solution: Local integration for refugees in developing countries (Working paper no. 45, new issues in refugee research). UNHCR, Massachusetts, USA
24. Janmyr M (2013) Protecting Civilians in refugee camps unable and unwilling states, UNHCR and international responsibility. Martinus Nijhoff Publishers, Leiden, The Netherlands
25. Jordanian INGO Forum (JIF) (2018) Syrian refugees in Jordan, a protection overview. JIF, Jordan
26. Jordanian Ministry of Planning and International Cooperation (MoPIC) (2020) Jordan response plan for the Syria crisis 2020–2022. UN & Jordan Response Platform. https://reliefweb.int/attachments/92c6ace6-2b18-3d73-b2bb-6160df18ec01/77970.pdf
27. Karsu O, Kara BY, Selvi B (2018) The refugee camp management: a general framework and a unifying decision-making model. J Human Logist Supply Chain Manage 9(2):131–150. https://doi.org/10.1108/JHLSCM-01-2018-0007
28. Kaya A (2023) Seeking asylum in the Middle East: lessons from the Syrian crisis. In: Triandafyllidou A (ed) Routledge handbook of immigration and refugee studies, 2nd edn. Routledge, New York, pp 396–404
29. Kingston LN (2019) Fully human: personhood, citizenship, and rights. Oxford University Press, USA
30. Koskenniemi M (2014) What is international law for? In: Evans MD (ed) International law, 4th edn. Oxford University Press, Oxford, UK, pp 29–53
31. Krafft C, Sieverding M, Salemi C, Keo C (2018) Syrian refugees in Jordan: demographics, livelihoods, education, and health (Working Paper 1184). Economic Research Forum, Giza, Egypt
32. Landini C (2021) Child marriage in the context of COVID-19: analysis of trends, programming and alternative approaches in the Middle East and North Africa. UNFPA & UNICEF. https://tinyurl.com/2mjatyz5
33. Library of Congress (2016) Refugee law and policy: Jordan. Retrieved from: https://www.loc.gov/law/help/refugee-law/jordan.php#_ftn6
34. Lipper R (1999) Governing refugees: the relevance of governmentality to understanding international refugee the regime. Alternatives 24(3):269–413. https://doi.org/10.1177/030437549902400302
35. Norwegian Refugee Council (NRC) & The Camp Management Project (CMP) (2008) Camp management toolkit. NRC & CMP, Oslo, Norway

36. Norwegian Refugee Council (NRC), & International Human Rights Clinic (IHRC) (2016) Securing status: Syrian refugees and the documentation of legal status, identity, and family relationships in Jordan. https://www.nrc.no/globalassets/pdf/reports/securing-status.pdf
37. Norwegian Refugee Council, Save the Children, Action Against Hunger, CARE International, the International Rescue Committee, & the Danish Refugee Council (2018) Dangerous ground—Syria's refugees face an uncertain future. Retrieved from: https://www.nrc.no/globalassets/pdf/reports/dangerous-ground---syrias-refugees-face-an-uncertain-future/dangerous-ground---syrian-refugees-face-an-uncertain-future.pdf
38. Office of the United Nations High Commissioner for Human Rights (OHCHR) (1979) Convention on the elimination of all forms of discrimination against women. New York, USA. Retrieved from: https://www.ohchr.org/Documents/ProfessionalInterest/cedaw.pdf
39. Peer S, Refugee Council of Australia (2011) Refugees. Hot Top Legal Issues Plain Lang 77:1–32. Legal Information Access Centre, Sydney, NSW
40. Phillips J (2011) Asylum seekers and refugees: what are the facts? Background note. Department of Parliamentary Services, Canberra, ACT
41. Rafferty Y (2013) International dimensions of discrimination and violence against girls: a human rights perspective. J Int Women's Stud 14(1):1–23
42. Su A (2017) Why Jordan is deporting Syrian refugees. The Atlantic. https://www.theatlantic.com/international/archive/2017/10/jordan-syrian-refugees-deportation/543057/
43. Sweis RF (2016) Jordan closes border to Syrian refugees after suicide car bomb kills 6. The New York Times. https://www.nytimes.com/2016/06/22/world/middleeast/jordan-syria-attack.html
44. The Sphere Project (2011) The sphere handbook: humanitarian charter and minimum standards in humanitarian response. The Sphere Project, UK
45. United Nations Children's Fund (UNICEF) (2005) Early marriage: a harmful traditional practice: a statistical exploration. UNICEF, New York, USA
46. United Nations Committee on the Elimination of Discrimination Against Women (CEDAW) (1994) CEDAW general recommendation no. 21: equality in marriage and family relations [UN Doc. A/49/38, Thirteenth session]
47. United Nations General Assembly (1948) Universal declaration of human rights. Retrieved from: http://www.ohchr.org/EN/UDHR/Documents/UDHR_Translations/eng.pdf
48. United Nations High Commissioner for Refugees (UNHCR) (1951) Convention relating to the status of refugees. In UNHCR (ed) Convention and protocol relating to the status of refugees (2011). UNHCR, Geneva, Switzerland, pp 13–45
49. United Nations High Commissioner for Refugees (UNHCR) (2001) Global consultation on international protection/third track: protection of refugees in mass influx situations: overall protection framework. Retrieved from: http://www.unhcr.org/protection/globalconsult/3ae68f3c24/protection-refugees-mass-influx-situations-overall-protection-framework.html
50. United Nations High Commissioner for Refugees (UNHCR) (2010) Convention and protocol relating to the status of refugees. UNHCR, Geneva, Switzerland
51. United Nations High Commissioner for Refugees (UNHCR) (2014) Policy on alternatives to camps. UNHCR, Geneva, Switzerland
52. United Nations High Commissioner for Refugees (UNHCR) (2015) UNHCR asylum trends 2014: level and trends in industrialised countries. UNHCR, Geneva, Switzerland
53. United Nations High Commissioner for Refugees (UNHCR) (2016) 'Refugees' and 'Migrants': frequently asked questions (FAQs). Retrieved from: http://www.unhcr.org/news/latest/2016/3/56e95c676/refugees-migrants-frequently-asked-questions-faqs.html
54. United Nations High Commissioner for Refugees (UNHCR) (2017) Protecting refugees: Cyprus. UNHCR Cyprus, Nicosia
55. United Nations High Commissioner for Refugees (UNHCR) (2020) Refugee registration and profiling in Jordan. https://reliefweb.int/attachments/e24adf85-641d-369b-8ead-a078f6ed4b51/73834.pdf
56. United Nations High Commissioner for Refugees (UNHCR) (2021) The 1951 refugee convention: 70 years of life-saving protection [Press release]. https://www.unhcr.org/news/news-releases/1951-refugee-convention-70-years-life-saving-protection

57. United Nations High Commissioner for Refugees (UNHCR) (2022) Durable solutions required for Syrian refugees in Jordan as Za'atari camp turns 10 [Briefing Note]. Retrieved from: https://www.unhcr.org/news/durable-solutions-required-syrian-refugees-jordan-zaatari-camp-turns-10
58. United Nations High Commissioner for Refugees (UNHCR) (2023) Registered people of concern refugees and asylum seekers in Jordan (as of 28 Feb 2023). Retrieved from: https://reliefweb.int/attachments/269c230c-ad0d-41c0-9d65-6ba71d6ab6b4/External%20Statistical%20Report%20on%20UNHCR%20Registered%20People%20Of%20Concern%20Jordan%20as%20of%2028%20February%202023.pdf
59. United Nations General Assembly (1962) Convention on consent to marriage, minimum age for marriage and registration of marriages [Resolution 1763 A (XVII)]. Retrieved from: https://www.ohchr.org/sites/default/files/convention.pdf
60. United Nations General Assembly (1989) Convention on the rights of the child (Treaty Series, 1577, 3). http://www.ohchr.org/Documents/ProfessionalInterest/crc.pdf
61. United Nations General Assembly (2000) Optional protocol to the convention on the rights of the child on the sale of children, child prostitution and child pornography. Retrieved from: http://www.ohchr.org/Documents/ProfessionalInterest/crc-sale.pdf

Chapter 4
International Human Rights Law: Frameworks and Responses

At its most basic definition, international human rights law is a body of international treaties. States who ratify international treaties assume the legal obligation and duty to adhere to the protection, respect, and fulfilment of human rights practices within its domestic jurisdictions under international law. When a state's domestic legislative measures have failed to comply with the standards set out in the human rights treaties, or have failed to address human rights abuses, international law serves to enforce human rights mechanisms at either the international or regional level to ensure a state is complying with its commitment to human rights [35]. While the prevalent nature of forced child marriages may be conceptualised as a failing on part of international laws to effectively protect refugee children, a less considered aspect of the nature of the problem is the 'universality' of international human rights laws, particularly within the Middle East. The concept of universality implies a global 'validity' and 'applicability' [43]. In the context of international law, universality signifies that all laws and treaties are thereby globally valid, inclusive, and binding on all states [39]. As will be presented in this chapter, however, international human rights laws are seen to have been formed by, and based on, Western frameworks of thought and conceptualisations of justice that largely exclude the possibility of regional (customary) regimes and laws [43]. It is on this basis that tensions regarding the way Arab states response to, and engage with, bodies of international law may be found.

The primary issue of consideration regarding international law is that of 'state sovereignty'. Prior to the adoption of the Universal Declaration of Human Rights (UDHR), the nation-state was the primary subject of international law which afforded it legal status and rights within the international area in comparison to individual human beings that were, arguably, merely 'objects' of international law [18]. This meant that states were not subjected to "unwanted external scrutiny or adjudication of its activities … within the bounds of its own territorial boundaries" ([37], p. 15). State sovereignty and territorial integrity were thus, to a certain extent, 'sacrosanct' [37]. The notion of state sovereignty is often justified within the scope of legal positivism

S. Strungaru, *The Hidden Child Brides of the Syrian Civil War*,
SpringerBriefs in Law, https://doi.org/10.1007/978-981-97-2159-7_4

(that is, to 'posit'). The most predominant tradition of legal positivism, based on 'social source thesis', suggests that laws are neither 'personal' nor 'universal' [27], rather, that legal systems emerge from a "history of practice rather than nature, grounded in the consensus of a specific political community with a shared historical past" ([27], p. 77). In this way, legal 'facts' are 'social facts', in that they describe a system of rules that bind together a particular community [27, 30]. Legal positivism thus suggests that the existence and normativity of a legal system is, in essence, based on the existence of a 'community' and social normativity [27]. Based on this perspective, international law articulates its own objective collective existence and validity, from "the will of this community of states" ([27], p. 77).

While human rights were largely absent within international political frameworks prior to the mid-twentieth century, key international movements nonetheless demonstrated concerns for the rights of humans prior to the emergence of the UN. Notable examples of such movements include the international requirement to care for wounded and sick combatants (mandated under the 1864 Geneva Convention); the prohibition of slavery (expressed within the 1815 Declaration Relative to the Universal Abolition of the Slave Trade), as well as, the prohibition of the international trafficking of women and children, as drafted in 1921 by the League of Nations [18]. Necessarily, the horrors of the Second World War following the atrocities committed by Nazi Germany against "millions of its own people with little interference from other nations" unveiled the flaws of the international order and, thus, prompted formal measures to be taken for the legal observance and protection of human rights, "without distinction to race, sex, language, or religion" ([18], p. 5). As discussed in the previous chapter, the UDHR is considered the foundation of international human rights law [38]. Proclaimed and adopted by the UN General Assembly in 1948, the UDHR significantly follows from the context of the UN Charter as the first universal statement to, firstly, formally declare the "fundamental human rights to which all human beings are entitled to" ([38], p. 24), and secondly, give human rights an "international dimension" no longer limited within the "exclusive jurisdiction of a state". Correspondingly, these international instruments designated the UN as the principal "legal authority to embark upon a codification of human rights" ([18], p. 5). Today, international human rights law is grounded in the International Bill of Human Rights. This consists of the UDHR together with the International Covenant on Civil and Political Rights (and its two Optional Protocols), and the International Covenant on Economic, Social and Cultural Rights.

Conceptually, international human rights law is largely rooted in the theory of natural law. The theory of natural law purports that there must be conceptual connection between law and morality [12]. This suggests that rules do not have legal 'validity', that is, they are not considered laws if they violate moral principles in one or more specific ways [12]. For Beyleveld and Brownsword [12], 'legal validity', therefore, equates 'moral legitimacy'. When World War I and II revealed, as Chinkin ([15], pp. 76–77) describes, "a moral abyss of excessive adherence to positivist law", proponents of natural law invigorated a revived approach to human rights discussions that sought to provide individuals with "a part in international politics and rights in international law, independently of his government" ([44], p. 7). The theory of natural law with regard to international human rights law, however, continues to raise questions about universal conceptualisations of 'rights' and 'morality', as well as, the legitimacy of "societal agreement on what constitutes the common good" ([15], pp. 76–77).

Arguably, international human rights law, as a branch of international law, presents a contradiction. As discussed, international law as a legal system was initially "created by, between, and for states" ([31], p. 97). It characteristically suggests a commitment and obligation to 'state sovereignty' and 'state voluntarism'. In this way, Megret ([31], p. 97) considers these concepts to be at odds with "the very idea and purpose of the human rights [project]", which is both "radical and revolutionary" and "very much geared towards redefining sovereignty". While legal commitments are not usually neutral within the language of international law, human rights obligations, on the other hand, possess a 'special character' [31]. Reference to the 'special character' of human rights law was first made by the International Court of Justice (ICJ) in its Advisory Opinion on the Reservations to the Genocide Convention. The convention asserts that states who ratify or become party to a human rights treaty convey that their (state) interests are not "of their own…nor can they speak of individual advantages or disadvantages, they merely have, one and all, a common interest" [28]. This is consistent with the idea, as Megret ([31], p. 100) suggests, that human rights "pre-exist its legal recognition". Contrastingly, Benhabib ([11], p. 693) argues that "beyond the moral duties we owe each other as humans", it is unlikely that, in the scope of realist ambitions, global obligations and engagements concerning human rights and justice between states will result in long-lasting projects of "mutual benefit and cooperation". For Benhabib ([11], p. 693), the contradiction between international law, generally, and international human rights law, specifically, thereby lies in the fact that states are "not merely instruments for the realisation of human rights globally", rather, "their existence is precisely what gives the value of justice its application". According to this view, citizens may, thus, be seen to be elements of "an institutional relation…that fill out the content of justice" ([11], p. 693).

4.1 The Westernisation of International Law

To understand the nature of international human rights law it is, in the first regard, necessary to understand law as conceptually lying between the concepts of 'power' and 'justice'. In the second regard, it is necessary to examine the 'international' component of international human rights law, and its cultural, historical, and socio political relativity [44]. Given the plethora of cultural and social diversity worldwide, the question, therefore, appropriately follows as to whether international human rights law is backed, even subtly, "by preponderant political power, reflecting deeper ethical, moral or religious values" ([20], p. 35). According to O'Rawe [37], this question may be answered by examining the 1948 UDHR, considered foundational to international human rights law. While the UDHR remains lauded for rejecting state-centric "opportunistic interpretations" of human rights, the historical context of the development of the instrument might inconspicuously suggest otherwise ([37], p. 21). For Shah ([42], p. 26), the UDHR is contextually "rooted in Western history" in light of its inauguration "in the aftermath of World War II". O'Rawe ([37], p. 21) expands upon this by adding that, in the aftermath of post-War global political and economic instabilities, the UDHR was formulated and appraised by a small portion of politically dominant states who found themselves in "superior bargaining positions to others in the "universal scheme of things"".

The unexpected rise of post-WWII superpowers, namely, the USA (Western bloc) and the Soviet Union (Eastern bloc), is also relevant in understanding the nuanced framework of the UDHR. According to O'Rawe [37], underneath the surface of the text, the UDHR represents political and ideological differences between the democratic USA and the communist Soviet Union which had become apparent in the post-World War II years. The tensions between these superpowers which developed into decades of restricted rivalry, known as the 'Cold War', would also impact standards of international human rights throughout the twentieth century. During the Cold War, the market economies (such as privately owned businesses) of the Western bloc "tended to put greater emphasis on civil and political rights" ([36], p. 8). Civil and political rights largely emphasise an individual person's right to participate in civil and political life without discrimination, such as through 'freedom of speech', 'right to assembly', and the 'right to fair trial' without being subjected to torture or inhumane punishment [36]. The centrally planned (government-owned) economies of the Eastern bloc during the Cold War, on the other hand, placed greater importance on economic, social, and cultural rights [36]. These rights largely pertain to the workplace, including the rights to equal pay for equal work, to join and form trade unions, and freedom from forced labour, family life, such as the protection of, and assistance to, the family, and rights to marriage; social security, specifically, protection in the event of unemployment, sickness, or old age; as well as, the right to adequate standard of living, such as access to housing, food, water, healthcare, and education [36]. The Eastern bloc's emphasis on economic, social, and cultural rights consequently led to the misinterpretation of these rights as being only 'collective' in nature, resemblant of communist systems of governance [36]. The Office of the United Nations High Commissioner for Human Rights (OHCHR) ([36], p. 8) clarified, that while these rights have a "collective dimension" requiring cooperative "public effort through the provision of resources", they are also individual rights.

While proponents of the UDHR argue that there is no distinction between, or prioritisation of these rights, the distinction emphasised by the opposing superpowers nonetheless largely influenced the development of international human rights legal instruments. In 1966 an eventual compromise led to the adoption of two international treaties (known as the 'International Covenants'): the International Covenant on Economic Social and Cultural Rights (ICESCR), and the International Covenant on Civil and Political Rights (ICCPR). Together with the UDHR, these subsequently formed the International Bill of Human Rights. Critics maintain, however, that the International Bill of Human Right is nevertheless "skewed in favour of Western notions of rights" ([37], p. 22). According to O'Rawe [37] this disparity is illustrated within the discourse of economic, social, and cultural rights which arguably requires, for the most part, a high level of financial and human investment for its full realisation [36]. The 'collective' assumptions of economic, social, and cultural rights, therefore, suggests individual's dependence on the organisation and resources of their state's government. In this way, non-Western or less economically developed states, are oftentimes not as qualified to support the *universality* of its objectives [37].

Ongoing issues and difficulties faced by numerous states, particularly within the Global South, including poverty, unjust regimes, and unfair trade, continue to impact state's full commitment and realisation of universal human rights. The effective application of human rights within individual states may be seen as being particularly problematic with regard to the notion of 'universality' of international laws. In other words, efforts to "globalise domestic interests" have largely failed to address the practical and basic needs of developing states ([37], p. 3). This is especially true of newly formed states following their independence from colonial empires, who have found themselves in positions of 'sovereign equality' at the seat of the United Nations, despite their economic, legal, political, and social limitations [37]. Notions surrounding the universality of human rights consequently suggests that international law has failed to ensure that human rights stand "the best chance possible of becoming ingrained in the psyche" of the world order" ([37], p. 3). Shah ([42], p. 36) refers to ongoing post-colonial issues within Western approaches to human rights as not only lacking 'historical perspective' but, also, due to what Shah [42] describes as 'Western blindness' to the continuing marginalisation and discrimination of minority populations, and "denial of the existences of human rights concerns" in their own Western societies.

As a result, Western societies have, throughout modern-history, attained a 'role-model' position globally while refusing, to a large extent, to acknowledge the progression and modern-day prosperity of their economies and societies as contingent upon historical human rights violations, such as colonialism, imperialism, the genocide of indigenous peoples, and slavery [42]. According to Shah ([42], p. 37), this is a "deliberate and cynical attempt" of Western governments to "evade the liabilities that attach to human rights violations" and assume responsibility in the assistance of nations experiencing poverty and undeveloped infrastructures, and coherent legal structures and system. Scholars like Shah [42] and Bielefeldt [13], thus, compel readers to question the extent in which human rights is a "Western construct with limited applicability" ([13], p. 100). Nonetheless, human rights cannot be completely disconnected from Occidental culture and history. At the same time, human rights ideas and practices should more comprehensively address the challenges of, what Donnelly ([20], p. 38) refers to, as "social-structural modernity". This idea suggests that international law should adapt and respond to threats to human rights associated with "modern markets and modern bureaucratic states" which collectively effects every part of the globe to a greater or lesser extent ([20], p. 37).

4.2 Middle Eastern Engagement and Approach

The responses and engagement of Middle Eastern states with international human rights law is relevant to the exploration of both the theoretical conceptualisation of the *universality* of human rights, and the practical application and implementation of human rights by these states. A discussion of the Middle East would not be complete, however, without the consideration and understanding of the role that the religious foundations and doctrines of Islam play within the social, cultural, political, and legal affairs of many majority-Muslim states and communities in the region. Islam is a critical institution within the Middle East influencing, to varying degrees, the private and public sectors that impact (both directly or indirectly) human rights responses in both conservative states, such as Saudi Arabia and Iran, as much as within more secular states, such as Türkiye [10]. According to Islamic scholar, Abdullahi Ahmed An-Na'im [10], the significance of Islam and Islamic *Sharia* law in Muslim-majority states within human rights and refugee studies is that religion has remained a fundamental institution within the Middle East that guides human belief systems and behaviours. Pertinent to earlier discussions regarding 'natural law' philosophies, Islam is, therefore, seen to be an integral part of Middle Eastern human rights norms. Modirzadeh ([33], cited in Baderin [10], p. 3) concurs, reminding us that "human rights discourse and Islamic legal discourse are powerful forces in the Muslim World".

For Arab states, international human rights conventions that are based on the foundational principle recognising the 'inherent dignity and of the equal and inalienable rights of all' [48], are, for the most part, accepted within domestic legal systems to the extent that that they do not contradict precepts proclaimed by *Sharia* law [9]. *Sharia* is a manual based on the collection of a body of religious Islamic texts, including the Quran (holy Islamic scripture) and the 'Sunnas' of the Islamic Prophet Muhammad (corpus of the sayings, practices, and traditions). Notably, *Sharia* law is heavily entrenched within modern family law with Arab states. Inextricably tied to the application of human rights laws, family law significantly reveals how Islamic values and principles continue to impact family structures throughout the Middle East, particularly with relation to women and gender rights [10]. Culture and religion are, in this regard, seen as mutually relevant to the ways in which Arab states engage with Western international human rights law, particularly in terms of agreeing upon gender equality and religious liberty [13]. Given that the basic features of the present-day application of *Sharia* law is traditionally rooted in the first centuries of Islamic history, it is not surprising that there would be an apparent conflict with modern human rights law which developed "roughly a millennium later" during an era of technological revolution ([13], p. 103).

This juxtaposition of human rights definitions and obligations, between the traditional and modern, the religious and the secular, carries mixed implications for the realisation of universal human rights obligations in the Middle East. Although "the high ethical standard of certain parts of Arab law" are credited as favourably aiding the development of modern human rights law ([9], p. 213), interpretations of concepts such as *jihad*—one of the key pillars of Islam subscribed to by "the vast majority of orthodox Muslim scholars…at least in theory" (p. 214)—are arguably deemed incompatible with the fundamental principles of modern liberal international law which espouse "peaceful coexistence between coequal states" (p. 214). The concept of *jihad* when translated literally means 'struggling'. It conveys in one sense, the sinful predisposition of man and the daily spiritual tribulations or 'struggles' an individual faces which can only be redeemed through God's grace and mercy (also referred to as 'greater Jihad'). The second aspect of *jihad* (known as the 'external' or 'lesser Jihad'), which has come to be synonymous with the term 'holy war', represents the Muslim's outwardly struggles, including defending one's faith and Muslim society [16]. The terms 'jihad' and 'holy war' have in the present-day garnered increasing attention, particularly among the West, due to its usage by militant or extremist Islamic terrorist groups or individuals, as seen with the rise of the Islamic State of Iraq and Syria (ISIS) in Syria during the civil war [16]. To this end, adversarial responses by Islamists may perceive international human rights as a characteristically "anti-Islamic agenda" ([10], p. 10). As a result, Muslim states may feel that this confrontation places them in a position to 'choose' between Islam and human rights of 'the West', thereby limiting possibilities for realising a "common ground between the two systems" and, thus, "eliminating the possibility of realising human rights within an Islamic dispensation" ([10], p. 10).

According to Arzt ([9], p. 205), the five most important principles within Islam with regard to human rights are: "dignity and brotherhood" (principle one),"equality among members of the community" regardless of race, colour, or class (principle two); "respect for the honour, reputation and family of each individual" (principle three); "the right for an individual to be presumed innocent until proved guilty" (principle four), and lastly, "individual freedom" (principle five). Islamic scholar Majid Khadduri notes, however, some of the theoretical inconsistencies of these principles with relation to their practical application. For example, Khadduri opines that principal one, and similarly, principle two (as noted above) were originally solely expressed for the preserve of those individuals and communities of Islamic faith [9]. Khadduri (cited in Arzt [9]) provides a further example with regard to the inherent inconsistencies of Islamic human rights vis-à-vis international human rights (such as the International Bill of Human Rights) with regard to principle five. For Khadduri (cited in Arzt [9], p. 205), principle five is the most debatable and difficult principle to "relate to the modern concept of freedom" on the basis that notions of individual freedom, that is 'free will', per the philosophies of natural law, are at odds with the Islamic doctrine that "all human acts are subject to God's will". Resembling a socialist conception of rights inextricably linked with duties, Islamic interpretations of freedom within *Sharia* law stipulate that individual freedom can, thus, only be manifested through one's obligation (duty) to act in accordance with the will of God [9], failure to accept this duty inhibits one from expressing their human right to freedom as it is deemed to "lack justification" (Said, [40] cited in Arzt [9], p. 206). Conceptually, what this suggests from a human rights perspective, is that individuals living under *Sharia* are, thereby, obligated by divine order to demonstrate active obedience to their state. Here, human beings are not autonomous entities but are, rather, an integral part of the Muslim state. These notions may be perceived as problematic when delineating the limits of the powers granted to the state over the individual, particularly concerning a country's rule of law and judicial independence. This point is particularly relevant with regard to systems for the protection of girls from forced marriage which will be discussed later in this chapter from a Jordanian context.

Yet, Arab states have not been absent from the development of the human rights initiatives seen today, but rather, have been notably involved in events that contributed to the adoption of the 1948 UDHR through its drafting, approval, and its later ratification stages. A particularly influential figure is Charles Malik, former Lebanese representative to the UN who was one of the two principal authors of the UDHR [49]. Although a Christian Arab, Malik worked closely alongside research assistants of Islamic experts during his tenure as Rapporteur of the Human Rights Commission, President of the Economic and Social Council, and later, as Chair and President of the Human Rights Commission, succeeding Eleanor Roosevelt [9]. Correspondingly, the Egyptian representative on the Third Committee (Social, Humanitarian, Cultural) on the UN General Assembly, in his consideration of the UDHR as an "authoritative interpretation of the UN Charter", expressed his belief that "the competence of the UN in the question of human rights was positive" ([9], p. 215). He strengthened his view by arguing that the provision of 'non-interference' by the UN within the "domestic jurisdiction of any state" ([45], art. 2, para. 7) "...could not be invoked by such competence when, by adoption of the UDHR, the question of human rights was no longer a matter of domestic but of international concern" ([9], p. 216).

Saudi Arabia's abstention during the 1948 UN General Assembly to adopt the UHDR is arguably one of the most referred to examples within literature regarding Muslim-majority state participation in the creation of international human rights standards. Although Saudi Arabia was the sole abstainer among Muslim-majority states, this case has resulted in an all too often generalised portrayal of consensus among Arab states [50]. Saudi Arabia's objection to the UDHR was specifically with regard to Article 18 which states an individual's right to "freedom of thought, conscience and religion...[and] freedom to change his religion or belief..." [48]. Then representative of Saudi Arabia, Jamil Baroody, based his contention on scriptures from the *Quran* referencing the concept of 'apostasy'—that is, the decree that "forbids a Muslim to change his faith" ([9], p. 216). Baroody argued that Article 18 would, therefore, directly impede upon the Muslim faith and "invite missionaries into the Arabian Peninsula" ([9], p. 216). Although several Middle East and North African states, including Egypt, Iran, Lebanon, Yemen, and Syria, agreed with Saudi Arabia's position, they nonetheless approved the UDHR [9]. Notably, Saudi Arabia voted in favour of the International Covenant for Civil and Political Rights (ICCPR) a few years later [50].

Equivalent Islamic instruments to the UDHR have, however, since developed and have been refined as a way to capture the ever-growing presence and impact of "Western material and technological innovations" in the Middle East, whilst also ensuring that a law fundamentally grounded on divine revelation is retained ([9], p. 228). The Arab Charter on Human Rights, for example, was adopted by the

Council of the League of Arab States in 2004, and later entered into force in 2008 [24]. Formed in 1945, the Council comprises of 22 member-states predominantly from the Middle East, but also from Asia and Africa. Its aim is to strengthen military and economic cooperation amongst its member-states [24]. The Arab Charter itself brought an additional dimension to the objectives of the organisation: it combined *Quranic* values and Islamic jurisprudence with "contemporary norms of human rights…reflected in International Covenants" to form a binding treaty ([24], p. 1). What makes the Arab Charter unique from other international human rights treaties can be seen within its preamble. The preamble of the Arab Charter not only affirms the Muslim faith and grounds human rights principles as divinely ordained, but significantly endorses the long cultural history of Arab states "which played a major role in disseminating centres of learning between the East and the West, thereby making it an international focal point for seekers of knowledge, culture and wisdom" [2]. While "rejecting all forms of racism and Zionism" [2], the Arab Charter is, according to Ghormade [24], primarily concerned with the protection of the rights of Arabs living in Israeli-occupied territories.

The main criticism of the Arab Charter is that it lacks an enforcement mechanism. Following suggestions from critiques for the creation of a mechanism to allow inter-state litigation, in 2014 the Arab League of States approved the 'Statute of the Arab Court of Human Rights'; this statute, however, requires seven states to ratify it before it can enter into force [5]. Despite Saudi Arabia being the only state so far to have ratified the Statute in 2016, the Statute nonetheless represents a significant step in the process of establishing an effective judicial regime in the region [5, 41]. Presently, seven human rights experts serve on the independent Arab Human Rights Committee (also known as the 'Charter Committee') who monitor and review compliance by those states who have ratified the Arab Charter. These states are expected to submit to the Charter Committee periodic reporting, as outlined in Article 48 [5, 17].

4.2.1 Jordan and the Legal Pluralism of Human Rights

Jordan's legal system, like many modern-day Arab states, may be seen as being characterised a legal juxtaposition, chiefly comprised by two conceptually different traditions. On the one hand, it is comprised of European legislature influencing, in most cases, 'criminal and civil codes'. On the other hand, Jordan's legal system is also based on Islamic laws which are predominantly assigned to 'personal status codes' regulating issues and processes of marriage, divorce, and inheritance, to name a few [51]. The Jordanian legal system maintains separate civil and religious court systems to appropriately draw on different sources of authority when dealing with various cases [3].[1] For Warrick ([51], p. 40), Jordan's pluralist legal system greatly illustrates the "legitimacy struggle" within the state. This particularly affects the ways in which

[1] Jordan also consists of a third separate military court, though for the purposes of this book's discussion, will not be discussed.

citizens' roles and rights, and relationship with society is constructed and understood in different, often conflicting and problematic, ways [51].

The distinct complexions of the two legal traditions are, however, not entirely autonomous, in that, 'Western' legal concepts often shape personal status codes, and Islamic principles often influence civil and criminal law. But how does Jordan's pluralist legal system enforce international laws? Efforts made by the Jordanian government to set up a Constitutional Court may be taken into consideration when examining the role of Jordanian courts, particularly in monitoring and applying international human rights legislation within its own domestic legal system. As an outcome of the 2011 revision and amendments of Jordan's 1952 Constitution, the Constitutional Court was officially established in 2012 as an independent judicial body mandated to specifically monitor the constitutionality of law in Jordan whose decisions are considered "final and binding on all [authorities]" [25]. Presently, however, the role of the Constitutional Court largely remains unclear [4, 23]. According to Aljaghoub ([4], p. 3), the 2011 amendment to the Jordanian Constitution did not "clearly entrust this Court with the competence to monitor the constitutionality of treaties". As well, there are presently no clear procedural provisions with regard to the nomination nor decision-making processes for elected Court members or representatives [23]. A decade since its establishment, women also remain observably underrepresented in the court system, with the first female judge having only been appointed in 2020 [23].

From a sociolegal perspective, further ambiguity is arguably observed regarding women's rights issues in Jordan. In recent years, Jordan has been praised by human rights representatives for its commitment to taking its international obligations 'seriously' [6, 22, 46]. Jordan has also been favourably recognised for being one of the first Arab countries to ratify several of the most major human rights treaties, including the 1979 Convention on the Elimination of all Forms of Discrimination Against Women (CEDAW) (Aljaghboub [4]). Notably, although Jordan ratified the CEDAW, it maintains reservations to several clauses within the treaty [including Article 9(2) and Article 16(1)(c), (d), and (g)], that grants the same rights and responsibilities to both men and women to pass their nationality to their children, during marriage and its dissolution, and in matters relating to children as parents [47]. Article 6 of the Jordanian Constitution (2011) also demonstrates the importance of human rights and equality amongst its citizenry before the law, regardless of 'race', 'language', or 'religion'. During the 2011 Royal Committee to review and revise the Jordanian Constitution, however, the Arab Women's Organisation (AWO) explicitly addressed the lack of reference to the word 'gender' within Article 6 [7]. Despite efforts and demands to explicitly include 'gender' within the article, and inclusively address gender discrimination or the prohibition thereof of discrimination against women within the text, the amended Constitution remains unchanged [7, 19, 47].

The Jordanian Constitution and the 2008 Family Protection Law No. 6 are, arguably, two of the most prominent binding frameworks within Jordan's national legal system with regard to the protection of women and girls against violence. These domestic frameworks are instrumental in establishing measures for the legal and social support for women in Jordan [8]. Ongoing cases of discrimination, and injustice and inequality, against women in Jordan, particularly those most vulnerable, such as girl brides, may be seen as occurring, to some extent, because of the Jordanian government's failure to incorporate the provisions of the CEDAW into its national legislation [7]. Promising discussions between King Abdullah II of Jordan and women's rights activists were held in 2011 with regard to CEDAW that centred on strategies for achieving reform and modernising processes in relation to women's rights in the state [7]; according to the AWO [7], however, this also led to an equally unconvincing outcome. Whilst His Majesty stated that he "sought a more effective role of women in the decision-making process and in the National Dialogue Committee", the AWO ([7], p. 16) notes that only 4 of the 52 National Dialogue Committee members, "comprising representatives from political parties, professional associations, civil society, youth and women's groups", were women. Women's limited participation within public and political spheres and decision-making roles, together with Jordan's existing discrepant national legislation, may, thus, be seen as contributing to ongoing gender inequalities and discriminatory gender roles within Jordan.

Noted within Article 1 of the Jordanian Constitution (2011), the Jordanian system of governance is "parliamentary with a hereditary monarchy". In terms of governance and jurisprudence, this means that the King of Jordan holds the highest authority to ratify and promulgate laws, and treaties and agreements [14]. The King also holds the overruling power to suspend or dissolve parliament or dismiss its parliamentarians (including the Prime Minister), suspend elections, grant special pardon or remit any sentence [4], as Supreme Commander of the Armed Forces, the King also holds the power to declare war and conclude peace [4]. As such, there is no reference within the Jordanian Constitution that establishes and mandates international treaties as higher authority than its domestic laws and powers granted to the reigning monarchy.

Furthermore, women in Jordan are significantly excluded from participation and representation within *Sharia* judicial courts and systems which consequently limits their capacity to protect their individual rights under personal status laws. As previously commented on, personal status laws in Jordan are highly entrenched and dependent on Islamic interpretations [8]. According to Jordanian activist, Rana Husseini, "*Sharia* courts do not treat women as equals before the law" ([19], online). Recent women's rights movements in Jordan, however, have emphasised women's empowerment in terms of 'equity' more so than equality, whilst advocating for the preservation and maintenance of social status laws traditionally based on *Sharia.* In other words, according to former Jordanian Member of Parliament, Dima Tahboub, equitable jurisprudence considers the best option for women to be productive and protected within society regardless of their social or economic status [19]. Necessarily, women's rights continue to be a contentious topic. Islamic conservatives, for example, not only associate women's rights with 'anti-Islam' or 'anti-national' movements but claim that international human rights instruments, such as the CEDAW, "violates *Sharia* law and enforces a Western agenda" ([19], online). These perceptions continue to consequently hinder any effective progress towards women's participation in Jordanian public and political life [8, 19].

Concerns about women's rights movements among conservative critics in Jordan are also characterised by a 'fear' of shifting demographics, particularly with relation to Palestinian refugees. According to Davis [19], these concerns particularly centre around Jordan's nationality law in which critics argue that increased women's rights will consequently expand citizenship eligibility to Palestinian refugees making Jordan their 'alternative homeland'. Presently, according to Jordanian nationality law, Jordanian women who are married to non-Jordanian men cannot legally pass their nationality to their children [1]. These concerns have, in recent years, also been noted of Syrian refugee women. The continued entry of predominantly Syrian refugees has placed considerable economic pressure on Jordan. In response, Jordan continues to receive international support and fiscal contributions to alleviate conditions allowing for greater response and action to be taken by the local government in terms of providing protection and opportunities for local Jordanian and Syrian refugee women and children. Despite Jordan's foreign aid assistance for the improvement of health and education institutions, such donations are often not conditional upon the state's domestic policies. This means that Jordan is not obligated (or under the condition) to enforce the terms of international treaties such as CEDAW within its domestic jurisdiction [8, 21, 22]. Notably, Syrian refugee women and girls fall under Jordanian legal jurisdictions and, thus, endure the same issues pertaining to personal status laws as Jordanian women [8, 29, 34].

Accountability and prosecution, or lack thereof, against perpetrators of sexual violence both inside and outside of refugee camps, for example, further reflects the discriminatory nature of Jordanian legislation and the "absence of effective implementation" international human rights instruments such as CEDAW ([8], p. 8). Child marriage remains one of the most concerning examples of the fluid nature of Jordanian laws, largely affecting Syrian refugees. While the legal age of marriage in Jordan is 18 years, Jordanian personal status law allows, under exceptional excuses, customary judges to consent to girls under the age of 16 to marry (subject to certain conditions) if the circumstance is deemed to be beneficial for the girl. As is often seen in cases of forced marriage among Syrian refugees, girls are married off to older men by their families in search of protection and financial support. Ironically, such scenarios, as discussed in Chapters Two and Three, only further contribute to a girl's vulnerability to sexual violence.

In this way, Jordan represents a unique perspective on legal pluralism. Jordan's legal frameworks interact with 'Western' and 'Arab' notions of human rights that provide different legal mechanisms. The pluralist legal systems of numerous Arab states in the Middle East, including Jordan, exemplify what ([52], p. 5) describes as "when a developed body of law is brought into a territory where it has not previously been observed". For Jordan in particular, rather than emulating a verbatim archetype of *Sharia*, its patrilineal nationality laws may instead be seen as being based on both early twentieth century British citizenship and nationality laws and Ottoman civil codes [22]. As seen, the demarcation between 'Western' and 'Middle Eastern' legal concepts is not so clear cut. For Hooker ([26], cited in Woodman [52], p. 5), modern-day systems of legal pluralism are largely the result of "the transfer of whole legal systems across cultural boundaries". In the context of human rights, present-day problems occurring in Jordan in relation to violence against women and girls through practices such as child marriage, may not necessarily be in relation to the "intractability of tradition but the disconnection between two different bases of authority" ([51], p. 39). National legislation and strategies are, thus, crucial in the harmonisation and application of human rights tools and services, all whilst benefitting from international frameworks and past experience to identify the best solutions.

As discussed, the concept of 'universality' of individual human rights, as espoused by international human rights instruments, are often in contradiction to the notion of state sovereignty. This contradiction is demonstrated in the case of Jordan where its legislative and judicial systems are characterised by both 'Western' and 'Arab' notions. The juxtaposition of human rights laws and obligations, between the traditional and modern, the religious and the secular, carries with it mixed implications. For Syrian refugee girls the result is that they will continue to be vulnerable and confronted by practices such as child marriage as long as this practice continues to be justified and exempted by religious or customary courts. As has been shown, there is a scarcity in the application of international conventions on women's and children's rights in Arab judicial decisions, which inevitably undermines efforts of human rights committees and instruments such as CEDAW to combat gender inequality and discrimination. For vulnerable girls and young women, the problem is unresolved and ongoing. Arguably, a state's failure to adhere to the instruments and conventions it ratifies, consequently demonstrates a failure on part of the UN and its role as a governing body to ensure the universal protection of all individuals, especially refugee children. Here, states are only required to submit periodic progress reports to the General Assembly, in a "no strings attached" arrangement, as described by Menz ([32], p. 22). While positing the failure of international mechanisms to protect vulnerable child refugees from forced marriage, the issue of 'Western' semantics of international human rights discourses and conventions needs to be contextualised in its application and engagements with Middle Eastern states if the practice of child marriage is to cease.

References

1. Al-Hashash FT (2023) The children of Jordanian women: citizens without real citizenship. Center for the Protection and Freedom of Journalists. Retrieved from: https://ammannet.net/english/children-jordanian-women-citizens-without-real-citizenship#google_vignette
2. Al-Midani MA, Cabanettes M, Akram SM (2006) Arab charter on human rights 2004. Boston Univ Int Law J 24(2):147–164
3. Alawad S (2012) Jordan court system. Rights Defenders Law Firm. Retrieved from: https://jordan-lawyer.com/2012/11/06/the-court-system-in-jordan/
4. Aljaghoub MM (2013) The implementation of human rights treaties by jordanian national courts: practice and prospects. In Novakovic M (ed) Basic concepts of public international law: monism and dualism. University of Belgrade, Serbia
5. Almutawa A (2021) The Arab court of human rights and the enforcement of the Arab charter on human rights. Hum Rights Law Rev 21(3):506–532. https://doi.org/10.1093/hrlr/ngab008

6. Arab News (2023) Head of UN's Palestine aid agency and Jordan's foreign minister discuss funding crisis. Arab News. https://www.arabnews.com/node/2341346/middle-east
7. Arab Women's Organisation (AWO) (2011) Substantive equality and non-discrimination in Jordan—shadow report submitted to CEDAW committee at the 51st session, Feb 2012. Retrieved from: https://tbinternet.ohchr.org/Treaties/CEDAW/Shared%20Documents/JOR/INT_CEDAW_NGO_JOR_51_9260_E.pdf
8. Arab Women's Organisation (AWO) (2013) Women's rights in Jordan [Universal Periodic Review submitted to the Human Rights Council]. Amman, Jordan. Retrieved from: https://upr doc.ohchr.org/uprweb/downloadfile.aspx?filename=538&file=EnglishTranslation
9. Arzt DE (1990) The application of international human rights law in Islamic states. Hum Rights Q 12(2):202–230
10. Baderin MA (2007) Islam and the realization of human rights in the Muslim world: a reflection on two essential approaches and two divergent perspectives. Muslim World J Hum Rights 4(1):1–25
11. Benhabib S (2009) Claiming rights across borders: international human rights and democratic sovereignty. Am Polit Sci Rev 103(4):691–704. https://doi.org/10.1017/S0003055409990
12. Beyleveld D, Brownsword R (1985) The practical difference between natural-law theory and legal positivism. Oxford J Legal Stud 5(1):1–32. http://www.jstor.org/stable/764429
13. Bielefeldt H (2000) "Western" versus "Islamic" human rights conceptions?: A critique of cultural essentialism in the discussion on human rights. Polit Theor 28(1):90–121
14. Bourouba S (2016) Arab jurisprudence in the application of international conventions on the rights of women: Algeria, Iraq, Jordan, Lebanon, Morocco, Palestine, and Tunisia. Raoul Wallenberg Institute, Sweden
15. Chinkin C (2014) Sources. In: Moeckli D, Shah S, Sivakumaran S (eds) International human rights law. Oxford University Press, Oxford, UK, pp 75–95
16. Cook D (2015) Understand jihad, 2nd edn. University of California Press, Oakland, USA
17. Council of the League of Arab States (2004) Arab charter on human rights [Unofficial Translation]. Retrieved from: https://digitallibrary.un.org/record/551368/files/%5BST_HR_%5DCHR_NONE_2004_40_Rev.1-EN.pdf?ln=en
18. Cumper P (1999) Human rights: history, development and classification. In: Hegarty A, Leonard S (eds) A human rights: an agenda for the 21st century. Cavendish Publishing Limited, London, UK, pp 1–9
19. Davis H (2022) 'Elephant in the room': Jordanian women and equal rights. Al Jazeera. https://aje.io/g2548g
20. Donnelly J (2010) International human rights: universal, relative or relatively universal? In: Ssenyonjo M, Baderin MA (eds) International human rights law: six decades after the UDHR and beyond. Ashgate Publishing Limited, Surrey, UK, pp 31–49
21. Douch M, Edwards H, Landman T, Mallick S (2022) Aid effectiveness: Human rights as a conditionality measure. World Dev 158:1–22. https://doi.org/10.1016/j.worlddev.2022.105978
22. Emanuel J (2012) Discriminatory nationality laws in Jordan and their effect on mixed refugee families (Report No. 2012–4, Unpublished). Retrieved from University of Notre Dame Law School, Indiana. https://www3.nd.edu/~ndlaw/prog-human-rights/student-research-pap ers/NationalityLawsInJordan.pdf
23. Eyadat Z, Nasrawin L (2021) The constitutional court of jordan: evaluating 10 years of service & future expectations. Konrad-Adenauer-Stiftung, Beirut, Lebanon
24. Ghormade V (2012) Analytical Framework of the protection of human right under the Arab charter on human rights (2004). Working Paper, Mzumbe University. SSRN. Retrieved from: https://papers.ssrn.com/sol3/papers.cfm?abstract_id=2000043
25. Government of Jordan (GoJ) (2011) Constitution of The Hashemite Kingdom of Jordan 1952, with amendment (Unofficial English Translation). Retrieved from: https://www.constitutepr oject.org/constitution/Jordan_2011
26. Hooker M B (1975). Legal pluralism: an introduction to colonial and neo-colonial laws. Oxford: Clarendon Press.

27. Hovell D (2022) The elements of international legal positivism. Curr Leg Probl 75(1):71–109. https://doi.org/10.1093/clp/cuac003
28. International Court of Justice (ICG) (1951). Reservation to the convention on the prevention and punishment of the crime of genocide (Advisory Opinion of May 28th, 1951). A. W. Sijthoff Publishing Company, Leiden, Holland
29. Landini C (2021) Child marriage in the context of COVID-19: analysis of trends, programming and alternative approaches in the Middle East and North Africa. UNFPA & UNICEF. https://tinyurl.com/2mjatyz5
30. Mazurkiewicz S (2019) Legal positivism social source thesis and metaphysical grounding: employing metaphysical grounding based on metaphysical laws. J Polish Sect IVR 2(20):5–19. https://doi.org/10.36280/AFPiFS.2019.2.5
31. Megret F (2014) Nature of obligations. In: Moeckli D, Shah S, Sivakumaran S (eds) International human rights law. Oxford University Press, Oxford, UK, pp 75–95
32. Menz S (2016) Stateless and child marriage as intersectional phenomena: instability, inequality, and the role of the international community. Calif Law Rev 104(2)
33. Modirzadeh N K (2006). Taking Islamic Law Seriously: INGOs and the Battle for Muslim Hearts and Minds', 19, Harvard Human Rights Journal, 192–233
34. Norweigian Refugee Council (NRC) & United Nations High Commissioner for Refugees (UNHCR) (2021) Legal identity and housing, land and property rights of Syrian refugees from a durable solutions perspective: challenges and opportunities. https://reliefweb.int/attachments/eccb44e1-bd21-3f62-b556-d7662cc56d8a/Legal_Identity_and_Housing_Land_and_Property_Rights.pdf
35. Office of the United Nations High Commissioner for Human Rights (OHCHR) (n.d.) International human rights law. Retrieved 15 July 2023, from: http://www.ohchr.org/EN/ProfessionalInterest/Pages/InternationalLaw.aspx
36. Office of the United Nations High Commissioner for Human Rights (OHCHR) (2008) Frequently asked questions on economic, social and cultural rights (Fact Sheet No. 33, Human Rights). OHCHR, Geneva, Switzerland
37. O'Rawe M (1999) The United Nations: structure versus substance (lessons from the principal treaties and covenants). In: Hegarty A, Leonard S (eds) A human rights: an agenda for the 21st century. Cavendish Publishing Limited, London, UK, pp 1–9
38. Peer S, Refugee Council of Australia (2011) Refugees. Hot Top Legal Issues Plain Lang 77:1–32. Legal Information Access Centre, Sydney, NSW
39. Riegner M (2012) How universal are international law and development? Engaging with postcolonial and Third World scholarship from the perspective of its other. Verfassung Und Recht in Übersee/Law Polit Africa, Asia Latin America 45(2):232–248. http://www.jstor.org/stable/43256854
40. Said Abdul-Aziz (1979). "Human Rights in Islamic Perspective". In A. Pollis and P. Schwab (eds.), Human Rights: Cultural and Ideological Perspectives, New York: Praege
41. Saudi Press Agency (2016) Arab league secretary general welcomes Saudi Arabia's ratification on the statute of Arab court for human rights. Saudi Press Agency. Retrieved from: https://sp.spa.gov.sa/viewfullstory.php?lang=en&newsid=1513644
42. Shah P (1997) International human rights: a perspective from India. Fordham Int Law J 21(1):24–44
43. Simma B (2009) Universality of international law from the perspective of a practitioner. Eur J Int Law 20(2):265–297. https://doi.org/10.1093/ejil/chp028
44. Ssenyonjo M, Baderin MA (eds) (2010) International human rights law: six decades after the UDHR and beyond. Ashgate Publishing Limited, Surrey, UK
45. United Nations (1945) Charter of the United Nations (1 UNTS XVI). Retrieved from: http://www.un.org/en/sections/un-charter/un-charter-full-text/
46. United Nations (2022) Jordan: UN expert lauds efforts on disability rights and encourages international support [Press Release]. UN. https://www.ohchr.org/en/press-releases/2022/09/jordan-un-expert-lauds-efforts-disability-rights-and-encourages

47. United Nations Population Fund, United Nations Development Programme, UN Women, & United Nations Economic and Social Commission for Western Asia (2019) Gender justice & the law: Jordan. Retrieved from: https://www.undp.org/sites/g/files/zskgke326/files/migration/arabstates/Jordan.Summary.19.Eng.pdf
48. United Nations General Assembly (1948) Universal declaration of human rights. http://www.ohchr.org/EN/UDHR/Documents/UDHR_Translations/eng.pdf
49. Verma R (2018) 70 Years on from the universal declaration of human rights, it's needed more than ever. Each other. Retrieved from: https://eachother.org.uk/70-years-on-from-the-universal-declaration-of-human-rights-its-needed-more-than-ever/
50. Waltz S (2004) Universal human rights: the contribution of Muslim states. Hum Rights Q 26(4):799–844
51. Warrick C (2009) Law in the service of legitimacy: gender and politics in Jordan. Ashgate Publishing Limited, Surrey, England
52. Woodman GR (1999) The idea of legal pluralism. In Dupret B, Berger M, al-Zwaini L (eds) Legal pluralism in the Arab world. Kluwer Law International, The Hague, pp 3–20

Chapter 5
The Future for Vulnerable Child Brides

The Syrian refugee crisis remains the largest displacement crisis in the world [34]. Significant concentrations of vulnerable Syrian refugees seeking asylum in neighbouring states has placed a high demand on host states such as Jordan, impacting the quality of services and exacerbating "pre-existing socioeconomic disparities" in the host nation ([20], p. 1). In addition to facing high levels of economic insecurity as the locals of the host-nation, Syrian refugees are also faced with the additional daily challenge of securing basic needs and accessing essential services and facilities because of their legal status. Difficulties associated with refugee identity registration and labour policies consequently impact Syrian refugees' residency, mobility, and finances [20]. Concerningly, Jordan's stringent identification requirements for obtaining residency permits (Ministry of Interior (MoI) cards) place Syrian refugee children, particularly girls, in precarious situations where they themselves are often the subjects of transactions involving "informal, sometimes unsafe, exploitative or dangerous work" ([20], p. 1). These transactions are often initiated by their parents in an effort to alleviate the living situation of refugee households. As illustrated in the Syrian refugee context, child marriage is often considered to be a means to offer the child protection and security, even though this is a strongly contested outcome [20].

What does the future look like for vulnerable child brides? This chapter explores two contrasting aspects of the notion of 'future'. The first aspect of future considers the effects and long-term impacts of child marriage on Syrian child brides' wellbeing and lives, respectively. It also explores the liminal situational and legal uncertainties of Syrian children's livelihoods in Jordan as refugees that both causes, and is further impacted by, forced child marriage. For Syrian child brides in Jordan, their futures are plagued with uncertainty and vulnerability. The second aspect of the notion of future explores international human rights' strategies and mechanisms to address the root causes of child marriage and end the practice once and for all. A future without child marriage means a world where more than half a million women and girls can have a better quality of life, agency and freedom to express their rights, and access to

S. Strungaru, *The Hidden Child Brides of the Syrian Civil War*,
SpringerBriefs in Law, https://doi.org/10.1007/978-981-97-2159-7_5

opportunities in public and private sectors. This outcome is only possible, however, through united efforts worldwide at both the macro international and state levels, and micro community and individual levels.

Child marriage is an international human rights violation. At its worst, "child marriage can be tantamount to bonded labour or enslavement … and a pathway to commercial exploitation" ([31], p. 11). The exploitative nature of forced marriages is often characterised by the adult roles and responsibilities child marriage prematurely imposes on child brides before she is considered mature enough to be able to provide consent, and physically, mentally, and emotionally prepared. The practice often forces girls into social isolation away from their family and communities, consequently impacting their access to social support networks, as well as educational opportunities and economic independence [13]. In situations where child brides are forced into social isolation, they are at high risk of gender-based violence, such as sexual abuse, by their spouses. Many girls are reluctant to report their abuse for fear of stigma or retribution, including damage to their family's 'honour'. Syrian refugee child brides, in particular, are also more likely not to report their abuse for fear of possible repercussions with relation to their residential status [10]. As well, girls themselves may be socialised into thinking that physical, sexual, and mental violence against them is inevitable or even justified. This is particularly seen within cases of child marriage where a girl's vulnerability to the risk of intimate partner violence flourishes, as noted by UNICEF [22], intimate partner violence is among the most common type of violence perpetrated against girls.

Subsequently, child marriage violates a girl's right to live their lives to their fullest potential and to express their views regarding decisions that will shape the entire course of their lives [25]. As has been discussed throughout this book, the consequences of bringing a girl's childhood and adolescence to an unnatural end through forced marriage practices are not only staggering but have lasting effects beyond adolescence which are often passed down generationally. One of the main impacts of child marriage is the denial of a girl's right to education and denial of her access to many of the long-term benefits which education yields, including empowerment and confidence to fully engage in society, and greater opportunities to develop skills for preparation into formal labour markets [15]. Without education, girls are generally more likely to also endure poverty and dire economic conditions, and be vulnerable to the exposure to exploitative labour, such as prostitution, as a means of providing for themselves and their families [15].

While child marriage was not uncommon in peacetime Syria, conflict and displacement in Syria because of the civil war has observably exacerbated pre-existing factors that caused this practice to begin with, such as, poverty, lack of education, and gender inequality [7]. For Syrian girls who experienced subordinate stigmatisation and treatment as 'second-class citizens' in their home country because of their gender before the civil war [35], conflict and displacement has only further demonstratively continued to contribute to the prevalence of sexual and gender-based violence, particularly within high-risk environments such as refugee camps. The United Nations International Strategy for Disaster Reduction et al. ([28], iv) succinctly conveys: "disasters don't discriminate, but people do … disasters reinforce, perpetuate and increase gender inequality, making bad situations worse for women". As seen in the context of the Syrian civil war, the resulting disruption on families, communities, and social structures caused by being forcibly displaced and then forcibly married, posit a sad existence for child brides that disrupts every aspect of their lives.

Child marriage among Middle Eastern refugees, including Syrian refugees, primarily occurs for three reasons. Firstly, it is regarded in some contexts as an appropriate traditional or customary practice by many Arab cultures. In these cultures, marriage is considered appropriate once a girl reaches 'maturity', typically marked by the onset of puberty and menstruation [18]. Moreover, there is often a preference for child brides because it is believed that "she will be easier to control" and that her physiological youth "will ensure more children are produced" (p. 12). Findings based on statements by female participants in their late teens and early 20 s within focus group discussions conducted by CARE International [18] revealed that "parents start repelling or rejecting older unmarried girls from the home, and some experience emotional abuse" (p. 7). Secondly, parents may resort to marriage believing it to be a way to protect their daughter from sexual harassment and violence. This justification is especially common within refugee camps where a child's protection against sexual abuse and rape is precarious, and where loss of the girl's virginity outside of marriage would severely damage her family's 'honour' [18]. Lastly, child marriage may be arranged to provide impoverished refugee families a source of income to reduce economic-related burdens in the household, particularly those associated with providing for the child. In this instance, the groom and his family are often customarily required to pay the child bride's family a 'bride price' (or dowry) in exchange for the marrying the girl [18].

Fundamentally, child marriage is internationally recognised as a form of gender-based violence. As noted within several key international law instruments, the practice is a consolidated expression of "gender inequality, abuse of power, and lack of respect for human rights" that are covertly institutionalised in social and political structures under the guise of culture and traditional norms ([18], p. 12). Whilst "conflict exacerbates vulnerabilities in the health, education and protection areas" the practice of child marriage fundamentally ensues "from a distorted gender environment" ([7], online). The "socially learnt dispositions" from their country of origin that have been "generated through normative performativity" continue to confront refugee women and girls across borders, as these structural hegemonies and hierarchies are reproduced and sustained within refugee communities ([3], p. 103). Here, Charles and Denman ([3], p. 103) purport that the trauma and loss experienced because of crisis, including "significant shifts in gender dynamics", may trigger for many men "hyper masculine associated codes of behaviour in an attempt to reassert normative gender roles". This may be particularly seen within refugee camps where the family unit is used as the primary system for organisation, and men assume increased patriarchal roles in the household [8]. Consequently, women's rights concerns and the implications of imposed unequal gender roles are often largely hidden and consigned "to the shadows of the private world and the periphery of refugee policy and practice" ([8], p. 4). While there are certain benefits to a familial refugee camp system, Indra ([8], p. 4), nonetheless asserts that these vulnerable environments can become "highly politicized along the lines of gender", consequently, public camp discourse regarding 'family' or collective 'refugee' concerns may "unilaterally reflect those of men". Here, gendered refugee discourse consequently fail to address the needs and required protections of most vulnerable cohorts within the host-state, such as refugee women and children, through effective laws and treaties.

One of the biggest issues endangering Syrian refugee children's protection in Jordan, is the inability to present required formal identification documentation to be registered as a refugee with the UNHCR, and subsequently, be issued with a Jordanian residence permit (MoI card). Without the necessary identification documents (such as birth certificates), children are *invisible* [21]. They are at risk of statelessness[1] and unable to access, among other things, healthcare services, education, and safe shelter outside of refugee camps (UNICEF & UNHCR [21]). The UNHCR has noted that a lack of civil status documentation is a "leading concern for conflict-affected ... families" ([27], p. 11). Notably, in the case of Syrian refugee children, their increased risk of statelessness may also be attributed to patrilineal Syrian nationality laws [14]. According to Syrian nationality laws, a child automatically acquires their Syrian nationality from their father, both inside and outside of Syria [14]. In the advent that a child's paternity is not legally established, nationality laws exceptionally allow for the child's nationality to be obtained through their mother [27]. This protection, however, is "only afforded to children born inside Syria", without exception ([27], p. 13). Where "the conflict has left one-fourth of Syrian refugee households with no father to attest [a child's] nationality", and without any records or documentation of their identity and parentage, children are, thus, at exceptional risk of being stateless ([27], p. 4).

The issue of statelessness faced by Syrian refugee children significantly reveals the persistence of established gendered nationality laws with predominantly Muslim-majority Arab states, and its intersection with the continuity of forced child marriage practices [12]. In this way, where the "systematic discrimination due to their lack of legal identity" leads to the "enhanced marginalisation and discrimination", girls may likely be pressured into marriage against their consent as a means of 'protection' ([12], p. 505). Such a situation, however, renders the girl bride dependent on her spouse, and unable to leave her husband for fear of statelessness. This inevitably places the child bride in a perpetual cycle of vulnerability whereby her movement and autonomy are severely restricted [12]. Conversely, marriage, in and of itself, may also leave a girl stateless. As presented earlier in this book, Syrian girls may be victims of temporary (or 'pleasure') marriages by typically wealthy older men

[1] For stateless people, the lack of a nationality deprives them of rights that the majority of the global population takes for granted. They are denied a legal identity at birth and often refused education and opportunity during childhood, and find themselves unable to marry or work legally in adulthood. Even the basic ability to reside lawfully in their countries of birth remains precarious. Available at https://www.refworld.org/pdfid/5829c32a4.pdf.

who later invalidate the marriage. As well, child marriages may be unofficially officiated by unauthorised individuals, such as lawyers, as opposed to sheikhs in *Sharia* courts, thereby leaving child brides without state-recognised legal protections [11, 17]. The risks associated with forced child marriage exemplifies how international human rights laws and instruments are failing to address and dismantle these gender inequalities whilst domestic citizenship and nationality laws continue to reinforce the idea that women and girls must be dependent on a male authority [12]. Here, child marriage illustrates how the practice exacerbates intersectional vulnerabilities, and impacts children within social, cultural, and legal contexts.

As presented throughout the book, the prevalence of child marriage arguably occurs due to a lack of law enforcement by international human rights bodies and institutions. While most countries, including Jordan, have ratified multiple international human rights conventions such as the Convention on the Rights of the Child (CRC), Convention on the Elimination of All Forms of Discrimination against Women (CEDAW), and the Universal Declaration on Human Rights (UDHR) which cooperatively mandate the need for mechanisms to protect children's rights, violence against children continues. This is particularly the case for Syrian refugee children. Syrian refugee children are trapped within a legal crossroads–between international and domestic laws, and 'Western' and 'Arab' (or 'customary') notions. Legal pluralism, as illustrated within Jordan's national legal system, often results in contradictory and negligent implementation and enforcement of protective international laws and policies within local systems of governance, particularly for those most vulnerable. For Indra [8], refugee laws are also highly gendered. According to Indra ([8], p. 3), there is a "systematic neglect of gender as a critical consideration in every facet of the refugee situation". Gendered refugee 'de-legitimisation' not only ideologically obscures "how different the refugee situation can be for women and men" and their "divergent relationships to the state and to the public realm", but practically places limitations on the processes and responses critical to the refugee plight ([8], p. 3). Here, the body of the 'refugee' is "far from politically neutral" but "remains primarily a male paradigm" ([8], p. 3). Until greater avenues of involvement are created for women to define and shape female perspectives and experiences in the refugee context, Syrian refugee women and girls will continue to be inevitably confronted with gender inequality in a "host country context and that of their source culture" ([8], p. 4).

There is some good news. There has been a steady, albeit slow, decline in child marriage over the past 25 years according to reports. In 1997, for example, it was estimated that 25% of women aged 20 to 24 years were married before the age of 18 [1]. By 2022, the figure is reported to have dropped to 19% [1]. This decline could be due to the hard work of advocates in this field. Presently, a global network of more than 1600 civil society organisations from over 95 countries work together in an effort to end the practice of child marriage globally [6]. One such organisation is 'Girls Not Brides' which was founded in 2011 by a group of independent world leaders, including the late Nelson Mandela, former President of Ireland, Mary Robinson, and former UN Secretary-General, Ban Ki-moon.

In 2015, 193 UN member states unanimously adopted a historic new global sustainable development agenda by 2030, referred to as the 'Sustainable Development Goals' (SDGs). The SDGs consist of a set of 17 goals that form part of an international 'Agenda in Action', as set by the United Nations General Assembly, which addresses "areas of critical importance for humanity and the planet" ([26], p. 1). These goals include efforts to limit worldwide poverty, hunger, and inequalities, to ensure good health and wellbeing, to ensure quality education, gender equality, decent work and economic growth, and peace, justice and strong institutions [26]. Significantly, the SDGs aim to address gaps between international and domestic child protection laws through strategies for the elimination of gender inequality, poverty, and the lack of economic and social opportunities for girls [5]. As discussed throughout this book, these issues are integral factors contributing to the practice of child marriage worldwide. Under Goal 5 of the UN 2030 Agenda to 'achieve gender equality and empower all women and girls', for example, target 5.3 specifically states the aim to "eliminate all harmful practices, such as child, early and forced marriage and female genital mutilations" ([26], p. 18). As such, the SDGs importantly reflect the collective drive of member states to ending child marriage. The realisation of these goals, however, requires a global commitment.

The year 2023 marks the halfway point to the 2030 deadline for achieving the SDGs. Despite global advances, a number of challenges to delivering on gender equality and, more specifically, ending child marriage, still remain [23, 32]. Presently, child marriage reductions are not occurring fast enough to be able to reach the current target [23]. According to UNICEF Senior Child Protection Advisor, Nankali Maksud, "we need to speed up progress to be nearly 20 times faster to reach the target of ending child marriage by 2030" [32]. UNICEF [24] estimates that if there is no reduction in global child marriages by 2030, "more than 120 million additional girls will marry before their 18th birthday"; this suggests that, at the current rate, "it will take another 300 years until child marriage is eliminated" [23]. As long as the practice of child marriage continues, the international community's ability to achieve eight of the 17 SGDs is hindered. For Lakshmi Sundaram, former Executive Director of Girls Not Brides, child marriage is, thus, not just "a niche issue; it's a key barrier stopping us from achieving half of our development goals" [4].

In response to the UN's adoption of the 2030 development agenda, the UNFPA, in collaboration with UNICEF launched in 2016 the 'Global Programme to End Child Marriage' in twelve countries where child marriage is most prevalent [32]. The program (currently in its second phase), consists of three phases [30]. Phase One (2016–2019) aimed to deliver quality services and opportunities for adolescent girls by strengthening institutions and systems in target locations. Some of the outcomes achieved by the UNFPA and UNICEF during Phase One include: the implementation of child marriage national action plans in 11 countries; outreach to 5.3 million individuals through community dialogue for social and behaviour change, and the strengthening of adolescent girl-friendly education in 26,000 schools [29]. Phase Two (2020–2023) accelerated actions to end child marriage through enhanced investments, improved reporting and investigations, and engagement with key actors to increase support, resources, and positive gender-response policies and frameworks

[30]. Some notable outcomes from the programme include, though are not limited to, the participation of over 60,000 community members in Sierra Leone in dialogues promoting gender equality, the participation of 57,000 girls in Nepal in life skills education, and the establishment of 1244 community welfare assistant committees in Zambia that reached over 13,000 adolescents [24]. Phase Three (2024–2030) is expected to enable longer-term gender transformations [30]. In 2023, for example, the UN sexual and reproductive health agency received a commitment of 35 million Canadian dollars to support the programme during the third phase [32].

At the regional level in the Middle East, steady progress by Jordan with relation to the rights of the child was also acknowledged by experts of the UN Committee on the Rights of the Child during its consideration of the sixth periodic report from Jordan in May 2023. One of the main outcomes, was Jordan's adoption of its landmark 'Child Rights Act of 2022' [19]. Described as a "truly pivotal moment for social justice in the country", the Jordanian Child Rights Act provides institutions and ministries in the educational, health, and law enforcement sectors clear guidelines for the treatment of children *with dignity*, to act in the best interests of the child [16]. The Act, however, lacks clear obligations against child marriage and discrimination of refuge and migrant children in Jordan [19]. As such, the dire need for clear and comprehensive legal frameworks to protect and address the needs of the world's most vulnerable cohort, remains imperative.

Failing to take into account the needs of refugee girls, and "failing to engage them in decisions that affect them" ([35], p. 13), Jordan's "nation-centred approach to citizenship" ultimately presents an "inevitable tension between sovereignty and individual rights" ([12], p. 506). For Warrick ([33], p. 39) the disconnect between the two bases of authority—the international and the domestic—is necessarily more problematic than of the "intractability of tradition". Legislative legitimacy must exist and be exercised within a meaningful socio-cultural context, one that reconciles authority and administration with "perceived social demands" ([33], p. 39). In the case of Jordan, harmonisation and compliance to significant international human rights instruments such as the CRC and CEDAW can only be achieved by considering its inclusivity within national legislation [2]. Even with such advocacy, without clear legal binding, and enforceable regulations, the practice of child marriage will continue within the "distorted gender environments" in which it currently occurs [7]. Looking forward, demographic trends and displacement due to the multifaceted nature of modern-day crises worldwide as witnessed in the last few years, including public health crises (as seen with the global coronavirus (COVID-19) pandemic), together with armed conflicts and climate change, continue to pose significant challenges for refugee children that place them at continued risk of child marriage and gender-based violence [23].

5.1 Conclusion

This book has sought to provide an overview of how and why the practice of forced child marriages occur among Syrian refugee children in Jordan by referring to international human rights laws through a sociolegal perspective. It has further sought to evaluate the effectiveness and limitations of international human rights laws in their implementation within the domestic legislations of Arab states, specifically Jordan. The primary aim of the book is to continue to raise awareness of the grave practice afflicting hundreds of thousands of children, particularly girls, worldwide. Until the practice ends, we as a human race, should never stop fighting for the rights and protections of those who are most vulnerable and voiceless.

This book has found that a juxtaposition of human rights definitions and obligations—between the traditional and modern, the religious and the secular—carry mixed implications for the realisation of universal human rights which consequently impact those most vulnerable, specifically child refugees. As a result, Syrian children exist in a precarious situation. They are living in a foreign state with an unclear legal status, are largely unidentified and, in effect, stateless. It is in this liminal space that Syrian children are vulnerable and voiceless, and at high risk of exposure to forced marriages and resultant abuse, trauma, and possibly death. While allowed to continue, the practice of child marriage not only severely impedes upon progressive international human rights efforts to eliminate gender-based violence, slavery, and discrimination, but significantly impacts on children's physical, mental, and emotional health, and their opportunities for growth and development in society.

Chapter One began by providing context to the research by introducing the body of the 'refugee' or 'exile', and the nature of mass displacement in the twentieth century which has arguably become a defining feature of the modern era. The chapter provided an overview of the conflict in Syria, deemed to have contributed to the largest refugee crises of the twenty-first century. The chapter also introduced the host-nation Jordan as the contextual focus within this study, and Jordan's response to the Syrian exodus. Jordan's relations with Syria, both as geographical neighbours, and in terms of close social, cultural, and political ties, are factors that have facilitated a large number of Syrians refugees to seek asylum in Jordan. The large influx and presence of Syrian refugees into Jordan, however, continues to impact Jordan's economy and infrastructure. Presently, Jordan is hosts the second largest number of refugees per capita worldwide.

Chapter Two introduced the practice of child marriage, both conceptually, and legally as a human rights violation within international law. It further examined literature on childhood vulnerability. The chapter revealed how children, particularly refugee children, or those in situations of conflict, displacement, and poverty, are amongst the most vulnerable, at the greatest risk of violence. As such, they are also in greatest need of protection. It also considered the concept of gendered vulnerability. Gendered vulnerability refers to ways in which social norms and practices reinforce constructions of gendered identities and sexuality that inevitably perpetuate gender inequality and discrimination. It considered how the sexualisation of girls makes them particularly vulnerable to harmful practices such as child marriage. Although both boys and girls are victim to forced marriage, the practice disproportionately affects girls worldwide.

Chapter Three presented the international and regional laws in place for the protection of refugees generally, and refugee children against child marriage, specifically. While Jordan has been praised for its progressive and 'hospitable' humanitarian stance on Syrian refugees, it lacks clear refugee-specific directives within its national legislative system. Jordan's unclear refugee policy framework, particularly by international refugee and human rights standards, continues to raise multiple concerns regarding its refugee practices and procedures, in relation, for example, to access of safe and affordable shelter, education, healthcare, and financial assistance. There are also concerns about their ability to protect refugees from harm and violence, especially pertaining to the identity regime introduced by Jordan under the guise of national security interests. This chapter revealed the discrepancies in Jordan's legal and governance mechanisms and frameworks to protect both camped and un-camped refugee children from sexual violence and child marriage. This is specifically evidenced in the lack of enforcement by international human rights bodies such as the UN regarding a state's obligations to adhere to ratified treaties, such as, the Convention on the Elimination of All Forms of Discrimination against Women (CEDAW).

Furthermore, Chapter Four analysed the emergence of international human rights law, specifically in relation to the issue of state sovereignty. It interrogated notions of 'universality' by presenting both Western and Arab notions and interpretations of human rights. This chapter culminates with the analysis of Jordan's pluralist legal system and what this means for woman and children's rights, particularly regarding personal status and nationality laws. Accordingly, this chapter illustrates that Jordan's legal frameworks combine both 'Western' and 'Arab' notions of human rights, that provide different, albeit conflicting, legal mechanisms. It has been argued that women and children's rights are largely referred and enacted within Jordan's gendered *Sharia* jurisdictions, which limits women's agency and presence within public and private sectors. Within the Jordanian legislative system, gender-based violence and practices like child marriage, thereby, remain largely unaddressed. Conclusively, this book has posited that international human rights law remain, to a large extent, ineffective, particularly for Syrian refugee children who are the main victims of human rights violations under weak legislatures.

The most significant conclusion that may be drawn from the research presented in this book is that the experiences and vulnerabilities of Syrian child refugees who have been displaced from their homes in Syria because of the civil war has a significantly gendered component. Forced marriages of Syrian refugee children illustrates, firstly, that child marriage is a form of gender-based violence. Secondly, it illustrates that refugee laws, policies, and directives are largely framed around masculine discourse which inevitably exclude female refugee experiences and female-based and led solutions and protections. Although international organisations remain active in their efforts to end the practice, child marriage continues to largely invisible to most of the global population. Ending sexual gender-based violence against women and girls must also be prioritised at the local and grassroots level—to change discriminatory norms and roles, strengthen protections and opportunities within institutions, and enable the voiceless and vulnerable to tell their stories and be heard.

The central aim of this book is to, therefore, contribute to the UN's international objectives of eliminating the practice of child marriage by 2030 through the Sustainable Development Agenda by increasing the dialogue on this insidious practice. As surmised by the International Center for Research on Women (ICRW) and the UN Children's Fund (UNICEF) ([9], p. 26), a key action required by both international and local institutions alike involves advancing gender equality to ensue girls "experience healthier, safer and more empowered life transitions whilst in control of their own destiny, including making choices and decisions about their education and sexuality and relationships".

References

1. Al Jazeera (2023) Child marriage rate falling too slowly, UN says in new report. Al Jazeera. Child marriage rate falling too slowly, UN says in new report | News | Al Jazeera
2. Arab Women's Organisation (AWO) (2011) Substantive equality and non-discrimination in Jordan—shadow report submitted to CEDAW committee at the 51st session, Feb 2012. Retrieved from: https://tbinternet.ohchr.org/Treaties/CEDAW/Shared%20Documents/JOR/INT_CEDAW_NGO_JOR_51_9260_E.pdf
3. Charles L, Denman K (2013) Syrian and Palestinian Syrian Refugees in Lebanon: the plight of women and children. J Int Women's Stud 14(5):96–111
4. Girls Not Brides (2015) Ending child marriage critical to achieving sustainable development goals, says girls not brides on international day of the girl child. ReliefWeb. Retrieved from: https://reliefweb.int/report/world/ending-child-marriage-critical-achieving-sustainable-development-goals-says-girls-not
5. Girls Not Brides (2020) SDGs and child marriage [Fact Sheet]. https://www.girlsnotbrides.org/documents/893/SDG-and-child-marriage_July-2020-update.pdf
6. Girls Not Brides (n.d.) About us. Retrieved 15 July 2023, from: https://www.girlsnotbrides.org/about-us/
7. Høvring R (2019) Child protection: what you need to know about Syrian child marriage. The Norwegian Council. Retrieved from: https://www.nrc.no/perspectives/2019/what-you-need-to-know-about-syrian-child-marriage/
8. Indra D (1987) Gender: a key dimension to the refugee experience. Refuge 6(3):3–4
9. International Centre for Research on Women (ICRW) & United Nations Children's Fund (UNICEF) (2017) Child Marriage in the middle East and North Africa. ICRW & UNICEF, Amman, Jordan
10. Know Violence in Childhood (2017) Ending violence in childhood: overview [Global Report 2017]. New Delhi, India
11. Laub K (2017) Spike in number of Syrian teens marrying as child brides in Jordan. The Independent. https://www.independent.co.uk/news/world/middle-east/child-brides-jordan-syrian-teenage-refugees-a7880831.html
12. Menz S (2016) Stateless and child marriage as intersectional phenomena: instability, inequality, and the role of the international community. Calif Law Rev 104(2)
13. Myers J (2013) Untying the knot: exploring early marriage in fragile states [Research Report]. World Vision UK, Milton Keynes, UK

14. Norwegian Refugee Council (NRC) (2021) The 2021 Syrian civil status law: implications for syrians living abroad. NRC. https://www.nrc.no/globalassets/pdf/reports/csl-syrians-living-abroad/nrc-csl-for-syrians-regional-report-en.pdf
15. Rafferty Y (2013) International dimensions of discrimination and violence against girls: a human rights perspective. J Int Women's Stud 14(1):1–23
16. Saqr R (2022) Jordan's child rights bill is finally here. Jordan News. https://www.jordannews.jo/Section-36/Opinion/Jordan-s-child-rights-bill-is-finally-here-18958
17. Save the Children (2014) Too young to wed: the growing problem of child marriage among Syrian girls in Jordan. Save the Children, London, UK
18. Spencer D (2015) "To protect her honour"—Child marriage in emergencies—the fatal confusion between protecting girls and sexual violence. In: Gender and protection in humanitarian contexts: critical issues series 1. Care International, UK
19. United Nations (UN) (2023) Experts of the committee on the rights of the child praise Jordan for adopting legislation on children's rights, raise questions about child marriage and discrimination against refugee and migrant children. Retrieved from: https://www.ohchr.org/en/news/2023/05/experts-committee-rights-child-praise-jordan-adopting-legislation-childrens-rights
20. United Nations Children's Fund (UNICEF) (2019) Syrian refugees [2019–2020 report]. Retrieved from: https://reliefweb.int/sites/reliefweb.int/files/resources/2019-HAC-Syrian-refugees.pdf
21. United Nations Children's Fund (UNICEF) & United Nations High Commissioner for Refugees (UNHCR) (2019) Being invisible: children living in statelessness. Retrieved from: https://www.unhcr.org/centralasia/wp-content/uploads/sites/75/2019/09/03_BEING-INVISIBLE-CHILDREN-LIVING-IN-STATELESSNESS.pdf
22. United Nations Children's Fund (UNICEF) (2022) Building back equal, with and for adolescent girls: a programme strategy for UNICEF 2022–2025. UNICEF, New York
23. United Nations Children's Fund (UNICEF) (2023) Is an end to child marriage within reach? Latest trends and future prospects (2023 update). UNICEF, New York
24. United Nations Children's Fund (UNICEF) (2023a) UNFPA-UNICEF global programme to end child marriage. Retrieved from: https://www.unicef.org/protection/unfpa-unicef-global-programme-end-child-marriage
25. United Nations Economic and Social Commission for Western Asia (ESCWA) (2015) Child marriage in humanitarian settings in the Arab region: dynamics, challenges and policy options. ESCWA, New York, USA
26. United Nations General Assembly (2015) Resolution adopted by the general assembly on 25 September 2015: transforming our world: the 2030 agenda for sustainable development [UN Doc. A/RES/70/1, Seventeenth session]
27. United Nations High Commissioner for Refugees (UNHCR) (2016) In search of solutions: addressing statelessness in the Middle East and North Africa. Author
28. United Nations International Strategy for Disaster Reduction (UNISDR), United Nations Development Project (UNDP), and International Union for Conservation of Nature (IUCN) (2009) Making disaster risk reduction gender-sensitive policy and practical guidelines. United Nations, Geneva, Switzerland
29. United Nations Population Fund (UNFPA) & United Nations Children's Fund (UNICEF) (2020) UNFPA–UNICEF global programme to end child marriage phase I report (2016–2019). https://www.unfpa.org/sites/default/files/pub-pdf/GP_2020_Phase_I_Report.pdf
30. United Nations Population Fund (UNFPA) & United Nations Children's Fund (UNICEF) (2021) Research strategy for phase II: the UNFPA–UNICEF global programme to end child marriage. https://reliefweb.int/attachments/2069f633-dd1d-3559-9c5d-0127e4bde0b7/Child-marriage-research-strategy-2021.pdf
31. United Nations Population Fund (UNFPA) (2012) Marrying too young: end child marriage. UNICEF, New York, USA
32. United Nations Population Fund (UNFPA) (2023) UNFPA and UNICEF welcome CA$ 35 million contribution from the Government of Canada to end child marriage [Press Release]. https://www.unfpa.org/press/unfpa-and-unicef-welcome-ca-35-million-contribution-govern

ment-canada-end-child-marriage?utm_source=miragenews&utm_medium=miragenews&utm_campaign=news
33. Warrick C (2009) Law in the service of legitimacy: gender and politics in Jordan. Ashgate Publishing Limited, Surrey, England
34. World Vision (2023) Syrian refugee crisis: facts, FAQs, and how to help. Retrieved from: https://www.worldvision.org/refugees-news-stories/syrian-refugee-crisis-facts
35. van der Gaag N (2013) Because I am a girl—the state of the world's girls 2013—In Double Jeopardy: adolescent girls and disasters. Plan International, Italy

SPRINGER NATURE

GPSR Compliance

The European Union's (EU) General Product Safety Regulation (GPSR) is a set of rules that requires consumer products to be safe and our obligations to ensure this.

If you have any concerns about our products, you can contact us on ProductSafety@springernature.com

In case Publisher is established outside the EU, the EU authorized representative is:

Springer Nature Customer Service Center GmbH
Europaplatz 3
69115 Heidelberg, Germany

The manufacturer's authorised representative in the EU is Springer Nature Customer Service Centre GmbH, Europaplatz 3, 69115 Heidelberg, Germany. If you have any concerns regarding our products, please contact ProductSafety@springernature.com

Printed and bound by CPI Group (UK) Ltd, Croydon, CR0 4YY
01/10/2026
02225839-0003